THE FAILED ASSASSINATION OF PSYCHOANALYSIS
The Rise and Fall of Cognitivism

Agnès Aflalo

Translation from French by A. R. Price

LONDON AND NEW YORK

Originally published in French in 2009 as *L'Assassinat manqué de la psychanalyse* by Éditions Cécile Defaut

First published 2015 by Karnac Books Ltd.

Published 2018 by Routledge
2 Park Square, Milton Park, Abingdon, Oxon OX14 4RN
711 Third Avenue, New York, NY 10017, USA

Routledge is an imprint of the Taylor & Francis Group, an informa business

Copyright © 2015 by Agnès Aflalo

The right of Agnès Aflalo to be identified as the author of this work has been asserted in accordance with §§ 77 and 78 of the Copyright Design and Patents Act 1988.

All rights reserved. No part of this book may be reprinted or reproduced or utilised in any form or by any electronic, mechanical, or other means, now known or hereafter invented, including photocopying and recording, or in any information storage or retrieval system, without permission in writing from the publishers.

Notice:
Product or corporate names may be trademarks or registered trademarks, and are used only for identification and explanation without intent to infringe.

British Library Cataloguing in Publication Data

A C.I.P. for this book is available from the British Library

ISBN-13: 9781782201649 (pbk)

Typeset by V Publishing Solutions Pvt Ltd., Chennai, India

In memory of Jacques Lacan

CONTENTS

ACKNOWLEDGEMENTS ix

ABOUT THE AUTHOR xi

PREFACE xiii
Bernard-Henri Lévy

CHAPTER ONE
The Amendment 1

CHAPTER TWO
Procrustes and the river of sludge I 19

CHAPTER THREE
Procrustes and the river of sludge II 35

CHAPTER FOUR
Cognitive-behavioural calculation 57

CHAPTER FIVE
Discipline and banish 81

CHAPTER SIX
Bioreligion 103

CHAPTER SEVEN
The commodification of knowledges 119

A FEW WORDS OF CONCLUSION 129

APPENDIX I
The new Amendment 131

APPENDIX II
"Scientifically" discrediting psychoanalysis and attacking civil liberties 135

NOTES 143

REFERENCES 149

INDEX 157

ACKNOWLEDGEMENTS

My thanks to Sylvie Lévy for her constant encouragement; to Anaëlle Lebovits for her critical reading; to Dan Arbib, Deborah Gutermann, Frédérique Bravin, Joachim Lebovits, Caroline Pauthe-Leduc, and Martin Quenehen for their attentive re-reading; to professor Emmanuel Lozerand whose remarks allowed me to add further precision to some points concerning Japan; and to François Ansermet for having included the French edition of this book in his collection at Éditions Cécile Defaut.

Lastly, Jacques-Alain Miller's *Lacanian Orientation* course played a decisive role in the desire to write this book. May he find testimony of my recognition herein.

ABOUT THE AUTHOR

Agnès Aflalo is a psychoanalyst, member of the École de la Cause freudienne and the World Association of Psychoanalysis. Her articles have appeared in various collections in French, and in *Hurly-Burly, The International Lacanian Journal of Psychoanalysis*. Since its first publication in French in 2009, *The Failed Assassination of Psychoanalysis* has been translated into English, Spanish, and Portuguese.

PREFACE

Bernard-Henri Lévy

This book had to be written.

First and foremost because it describes a battle of ideas that was waged some years ago now in France and whose full importance has scarcely been measured.

But also because beyond the particularities of this battle, and over and above its inherent logic and what came to be at stake in it, this book uncovers an emerging ideology whose noxiousness has hardly been measured any better.

As far as the first point is concerned, it is quite simple.

Agnès Aflalo is the first to have gone back over the history of those few very peculiar months that saw, as she says, an assassination attempt upon psychoanalysis *per se*.

It all began on 8th October 2003, with an Amendment put to the French Parliament by a *député* who was completely unknown at the time, Bernard Accoyer, claiming to "regulate" the profession of psychoanalysis.

A movement of public opinion fell in behind him, drawing on a stock of prejudices as old as psychoanalysis itself, and set about explaining how it wasn't normal for people to entrust their mental health to poorly trained or untrained individuals whose practice was not subject to transparent rules familiar to all and sundry.

Practitioners were found who, seeing the long-coveted chance to settle old scores, were happy to arbitrate age-old quarrels and give vent, out in the open as we saw with the likes of Daniel Widlöcher, to the hatred they had always secretly harboured for a certain Dr Jacques Lacan. This hate was inspired by Lacan's brilliant loyalty to the psychoanalytic legacy and by his scientific rigour, unencumbered as it is by any scientism whatsoever. The said practitioners were to lend their support to an attempt at brainwashing whose only possible outcome would be to transform the "shrinks" (psychoanalysts, psychotherapists, psychologists, and so on) into a body of prefects of the soul. These prefects would be trained by the state, answerable to the state, and would participate in managing not only individual bodies and souls but, more comprehensively, the social body, in a form that was to be willed and implemented by the state.

Over those months, this support was given with the idea of wiping out the singularity of the analytic discourse and analytic practice; of integrating the analysts back into the field of a medical knowledge from which Freud, and especially Lacan, had expressly, praise be, extracted them; and of making people forget, for example, that any notion of mental health, recovery, and pathology is strictly meaningless for an unconditional Freudian. Once again, all of this was to the delight of a power that would thereby possess the means to extend its empire over a region of Being that, since it coincides with the most intimate zones, since it overlaps with the specific relation to truth and to the painful aspect of truth that is specific to each speaking subject, and since ultimately its intrigue has no other thread with which to weave itself than the committed and enigmatic relationship between a subject and his neighbour, in the secrecy of souls, stood as one of the few regions to have endured outside its widely cast net.

As Agnès Aflalo relates, it would not have taken much for this offensive to triumph.

It would have taken very little for enlightened public opinion to be submerged by this populism crossed with positivism and the hatred of thought.

How about this "very little"? It met resistance from a handful of psychoanalysts who refuse to give ground when it comes to the straightforward idea that the unconscious is structured like a language and has scarcely anything to do with the molecular and cerebral chemistry to which neo-cognitivists claim to reduce it.

Then came reinforcement from intellectuals like Philippe Sollers, Jean-Claude Milner, Catherine Clément, and myself, who grasped that what was being played out in this attempt to absorb psychoanalysis back into psychology, and in the eagerness to reduce the body and its symptoms to a pure parcel of matter bearing the vulgar title "organism", went far beyond the analytic community and touched on the very idea of what it means to be human and the possibility of human freedom.

There was also a courageous Minister for Health, Philippe Douste-Blazy, who in February 2005, at one of the *Forums des Psys* that were held on a regular basis throughout this period, forswore the report prepared by Inserm, France's National Institute for Healthcare and Medical Research, which presented mental suffering as measurable data, as a magnitude that could be evaluated, and as a disturbance that the universal eagerness to cure would be able to bring back into line, reduce, and thus "remedy".

And then there was one man, one of the great figures of my generation, who for decades had only been giving us an inkling of what he was up to from afar, discreetly, through his editorial work on the oeuvre of another (again Jacques Lacan), and who seemed to have devoted his life to a selflessness, to an abnegation, and ultimately to a humility that had always struck me as enigmatic—a man who, perceiving in these manoeuvres a new episode in the long war waged against Freudianism by the mechanics of the soul, and against the teaching of the author of the *Seminar* by a number of supposed Freudians, found again the spirit of anger and revolt, not to mention the political mind, of his Maoist youth: to stand up against villainy; to set alarm bells ringing across town and city and further afield; to lead, encourage, and sustain the famous Forums that stood as intelligent mass demonstrations exposing, amongst other things, the power of resentment lurking in those who dreamt only of outlawing this Freudianism of such great consequence (the only one perhaps?) that Lacanianism is.

Sometimes history hangs on a thread.

It is quite likely that in this affair the thread bears the name of this one man: Jacques-Alain Miller.

But the second point is even more pivotal.

And once again the value of this book is to have set it out clearly and forcefully.

Did everything begin with this attempt to kill off psychoanalysis or was this failed attempt already the sign of a discontent that would not speak its name? I cannot say. But one would have to be deaf—and the least one can say is that deaf, Agnès Aflalo is not—to fail to perceive, right here, in the guise of cognitivism and its by-products, under the cover of a language that is at once newfangled yet utterly old-fashioned, where the most obtuse scientism argued in its favour with a "good" sense that was as simple-minded as could be, the implantation of a whole new ideology of which psychoanalysis was the first victim, though certainly not the only one.

Agnès Aflalo, and others with her, calls this ideology the *ideology of evaluation*.

This ideology leans on one postulate: that man is computable, that he is an object of measure through and through, body and soul pound for pound, mental and physical suffering alike, the whole adventure of thought, and that, beyond this, subjectification too is calculable inasmuch as it may be reduced to an abstract piece of machinery with cogs that hold no mystery—a kind of hermeneutics run amok, founded on the utopia of total meaning with no leftover, purged of the very shadow, opacity and meaninglessness that are part and parcel of what we are.

This postulate itself presupposes a regression that, ten or twenty years hence, would have seemed strictly unthinkable for any moderately enlightened mind. It fails to heed the very movement that was constitutive of modernity, by which:

a. science forgoes wanting to know anything about the "qualities" of Being, contrary to its ambition in the time of Aristotle and Plato;
b. it chooses to concentrate on what, in this Being, falls under the heading of "quantity" and allows itself to be reduced to a carefully ordered combinatory of numbers and letters;
c. it makes way for a site (as with Kant in his famous, founding critical gesture that limited knowledge in order to make room for faith) dedicated to a second sort of knowing that may be metaphysics, poetry or—why not?—psychoanalysis.

This regression is a kind of hystericised Galileism, which too has gone off the rails, because it has been won over by the demon of the canon, integral commensurability, and all-pervasive exchange.

By the same stroke, this regression brings with it a consequence that has a constitutive role in the *ideology of evaluation*: transforming the subject into an object; reducing the infinite diversity of subjects into a mass that is not exactly undifferentiated but in which one is only differentiated by imperceptible increments; in other words, ensuring the triumph of the man without *qualities* who no longer amounts to anything but *quantities*, heralded by Robert Musil but whose birth and reign, one century on, it has fallen to our era to foster.

This is the ideology that drives those who evaluate the "cost" of health care in a democracy, and who conclude, for example, that it would be better to pension off a sick man than treat him.

This is the ideology at work behind the pedagogical practices that have been cropping up hither and thither, assigning schools the task of detecting the potential delinquent in the youngest of children, and treating their latent criminality.

As I write, it is against this ideology that French researchers and academics have been fighting in their struggle against the Pécresse Reform, that is to say, to put it unambiguously, against the readiness to classify discourses and, in particular, the discourses of truth, by the number of articles published by the researcher, the number of pages in each article, the number of quotes or quotes of quotes from these articles, or the number of copies of journals in print in which these articles have been quoted—the Google method applied to the life of the mind. So it is that, if we look closely, a talk by a September 11th revisionist turns out to be better ranked than one by a social sciences scholar that has been less abundantly "clicked" and visited. With the dummy who numbers, classifies, and ranks, who snatches hold of all that is keen and vivid in a research project and punches it into a software programme that spits out bibliometric datasheets—*publish or perish*—doesn't the researcher become a kind of automaton who is asked to produce for the sake of producing, in serial form, on a production line, without any other concern besides putting out a specific quantity of knowledge, whether original or not, as required by all-powerful evaluators who are never themselves evaluated?

For the least merit of any book lies precisely in not providing the theoretical matrix, nor bearing the fruit, of these sundry practices of evaluation.

This matrix is a hysteria of the numerical figure; an idolatry of the number; the technical dimension edging into the last few domains that still resist it; in a word, the triumph of nihilism and perhaps—who knows?—its supreme stage.

What results from this is a humanity indexed on this technological vision of the world; a limitless extension of the imperative for transparency, which is thus an imperative for purity, and which I have long been diagnosing as the ultimate goal of modern powers; in other words, the appearance of machines of government that, leaning on the "good" they are supposed to bring to subjects by making them transparent to themselves and to others, gently force their consent or, if "need be", simply do without it; in short, the advent of a form of servitude, be it willing or unwilling, that feeds on charlatanism and revives it without letup.

Precisely because it finds the words and the actions with which to unmask this imposture, this book is a liberating book.

Precisely because it brings us not only the code to this new machine, but also some of the tools that enable us to jam it, it is a resister's bible.

All those who, with their eyes fixed on antique modes of tyranny, run the risk of failing to recognise the decidedly human face that tyranny is putting on today, would do well to read this book. In it they will find an arsenal brimming with the necessary weapons for the counteroffensive that is now due.

CHAPTER ONE

The Amendment

> Everything that fails to kill us can only make us stronger.
>
> —F. Nietzsche, *Twilight of the Idols*

The failed assassination

The "Accoyer Amendment" was passed on 8th October 2003.[1] It claimed to introduce regulation of the exercise of psychotherapies, but did so without any prior consultation, thus spelling a threat for the future of psychoanalysis in France. Indeed, within the space of a few days, a huge movement of public opinion led by Jacques-Alain Miller[2] had come out to express its great concern up and down the country. This movement saw several phases of intense mobilisation, the first of which lasted until Easter 2004, that is, until shortly after the Amendment went before the French Senate, at which time Inserm[3] had just brought down public wrath by openly siding against psychoanalysis. It was during these months, from October 2003 to Easter 2004, that the failed assassination of psychoanalysis was perpetrated.

This moment is well worth examining because psychoanalysis is a public good and it deserves to remain one. Yet, since 2003, the determination of its adversaries has continued to make itself felt, not only with respect to the Amendment, with its *décrets d'application* and other decrees, but also through publications that are hostile to psychoanalysis and which have usurped the term "science" with a view to using it to their advantage. Furthermore, to come back to this attack on psychoanalysis is also to show how these false forms of knowledge, which are exceedingly seductive on account of their scientific allure, could well come to enslave our democracies if adequate care is not taken. The history of the twentieth century harbours a painful memory of one such seduction. So, shedding light on this historic moment and specifying what is at stake in it is no small matter.

Psychoanalysis came into existence at the start of the twentieth century. That is a fact. Since then, it has continued to spawn a long line of different types of psychotherapy. Most of them have only maintained a small portion of psychoanalysis. They do purport, however, as does psychoanalysis itself, to be serious in their theoretical lucubration. Things had doubtless evolved a great deal since the beginning of the last century, but right up until the new millennium, never once was the practice of psychotherapies regulated. Passing the Amendment was the sign that this period was over once and for all. To begin with, psychoanalysis had been fairly hush-hush; it attracted only a wealthy few. Later it became far more democratic, to the point that "going to see a shrink" became fairly commonplace. This practice is still in vogue today because it corresponds to a deep desire, even though some find it hard to get their bearings amid the different shrinks where the "psych-" prefix abounds: psychoanalysts, psychiatrists, psychologists, psychotherapists, and so on.

Psychoanalysis was born in Europe. Next it spread to the New World and it was above all these new continents that saw the patching together of multiform variants of psychotherapy, before making its way back to Europe. The renown of psychoanalysis rubbed off on its derivative psychotherapies, to the point that psychoanalysis became a victim of its own success: the sprawling "shrink sensation" first gave rise to a market of psychotherapies, which then in turn tended to efface the singularity of psychoanalysis. With hindsight, we must acknowledge that the psychoanalysts didn't see this coming in time, or else, which boils down to the same thing, they didn't know how to draw the necessary conclusions from it in such a way as to orient their action. It was quite predictable, however, that the psychotherapy market would end up attracting the interest of Trusts, and that governments would be calling the psychotherapies to account. Yet, at the time the Amendment reared its head, not one serious incident in psychotherapy had ever been reported in the media, and thus the reason behind the absence of consultation leading up to the vote in the National Assembly remained obscure.[4] Why was it so urgent to "seal this legal loophole"?[5]

Beyond the legitimate question from the legislator, it very quickly became apparent that, under cover of "reassuring the general public", this was in reality about seizing hold of public freedoms. Indeed, the consequences of the so-called expert knowledge that had served as the Amendment's "scientific" guarantee amounted to just that. This knowledge emanated from a close-knit academic clique who for three years had been launching a large-scale editorial offensive with the objective of having its obscurantist discourse triumph over psychoanalysis. Once the alarm bells had been sounded, it soon became clear that the Amendment was just the tip of the iceberg. It was part and parcel of a strategy that was now plainly legible. The editorial offensive had consisted in readying the ground by scientifically discrediting Lacanian psychoanalysis with an eye to taking the next step of getting legislators to outlaw it by decree. This unprecedented attack on psychoanalysis shook the therapists to the core and brought a lasting reconfiguration to their world. The dividing line was no longer drawn between the psychoanalysts and the rest, but between those for whom speech must remain free and the others. To form some idea of the events that whipped up this struggle, it is worthwhile calling to mind a few dates.

On 2nd October 2003, the Ministry of Health issued a statement announcing a "Comprehensive Mental Healthcare Policy" put together on the basis of the roadmap drawn up by Dr Cléry-Melin. The consultation that preceded it had excluded all representatives of psychoanalysis, clinical psychology, and the psychotherapies.[6] With neither prior public debate nor dialogue with the professionals concerned, the deputies who passed the Amendment a few days later had not been informed of the role that the French Ministry for Health had given to the "Cléry-Melin Roadmap". This vote thus constituted in itself what was keenly identified by philosopher Yves-Charles Zarka as a "pathology of democracy" (Zarka, 2003).

At the end of October 2003, having been informed of the above by a major daily newspaper that was asking his opinion on the matter, Jacques-Alain Miller lost no time in giving the alert. No one had noticed the "Cléry-Melin Roadmap" until after the Amendment was passed. Some swift research from Dr Sophie Bialek and Dr Pierre Sidon brought to light the fact that the roadmap and the Amendment were two faces of one and the same project. In the Cléry-Melin report, the evaluation of the psychotherapies and their medical supervision constituted not only an infringement on the exercise of psychoanalysis, but also a breach of civil liberties. The report established a systematic bleeding of "mental healthcare" in France and its subordination to medical power. It set out how psychiatrists would become regional coordinators and decide authoritatively which kind of therapist a citizen should consult. Speaking to a therapist on order does not, of course, have the same effects as speaking to a therapist because one desires to do so.[7] Gripped by the dangerous prospect of a society in which psychiatrists would become "prefects of the soul", Bernard-Henri Lévy voiced his concern by throwing himself into an immediate and lasting engagement, shoulder to shoulder with the psychoanalysts in this enlightenment struggle,[8] in keeping with his duty as a philosopher, entering the fray of public debate to ensure that philosophy remains "an instrument for lucidity". Psychoanalysis owes him a great deal.

Through until February 2004, a series of fortnightly Forums were held, each bringing together over 1500 people, first in Paris and then, later, in the provinces. A number of intellectuals from all sides engaged in the battle. The writer Philippe Sollers, an ally from the start, put his renown in the service of the analytic cause without hesitation. The philosopher Jean-Claude Milner, who used to attend Lacan's seminars, also came forward, as did the courageous and committed intellectual Catherine Clément, along with many others, including: Roland Castro, Gérard Miller, Élisabeth Roudinesco, Maître Charrière-Bournazel, Maître Lévy, and other younger contributors such as Anaëlle Lebovits who had just created the group DIX-IT, Raphaël Glucksmann, and Alexandre Renault, to name but a few. Personalities from what we may fittingly call "enlightened public opinion", such as Françoise Castro, also addressed the public. Politicians from all the major parties participated in the Forums: François Bayrou, Renauld Dutreil, Jean-Michel Fourgous, Robert Hue, Bernard Kouchner, Jack Lang, Jack Ralite, and Jean-Pierre Sueur among them. Men and women from the world of arts and entertainment also contributed: Arielle Dombasle, Anne-Lise Heimburger, Brigitte Jacques-Wajcman, Gérard Pape, Marie-France Pisier, Andrée Putman, Jean-Pierre Raynaud, Pablo Reinoso, Irina

Solano, and many more. Journalists from the press, radio and television were present: Jean-Pierre Elkabbach chaired debates, and Edwy Plenel took the floor. The events were covered by Jean Birnbaum, Éric Favereau, Maurice Szafran, Cécile Prieur and Catherine Petitnicolas, amongst others. Some of them published articles in the major broadsheets and weekly news magazines, but also in the journal *Le Nouvel Âne*. The offensive stood as a declaration of war on psychoanalysis, but once it was seen to be infringing upon freedoms it also provoked a debate on the kind of society we live in, with, at the heart of the torment, the "steering state" and its demand for scientistic evaluation.

Mid-November 2003 saw the drafting of a manifesto, the *Manifeste Psy*,[9] bringing together practitioners of all persuasions: psychoanalysts, psychotherapists, clinical psychologists, and psychiatrists. It called for a retraction of the 2nd October Ministry of Health statement and a freeze on the Accoyer Amendment. Considering the "Accoyer/Cléry-Melin" project to be a breach of civil liberties and privacy, a joint committee was set up, the *Coordination Psy*, proposing a declaration that established two principles: the right of the suffering person to choose his or her own therapist without state interference, and the duty of therapists to stand before the public as guarantors, via their associations and schools.

By the end of November 2003, more than 3000 people had called either for the withdrawal of the Accoyer Amendment or for it to be modified after a debate between the psychoanalytic associations, the elected representatives, and the ministers concerned.

At the start of December 2003, different personalities from the political sphere were showing signs of appeasement. Laurent Fabius asked then Prime Minister Jean-Pierre Raffarin to withdraw the Accoyer Amendment and initiate a dialogue. Bernard Accoyer himself acknowledged that several clauses in the Amendment could be revised. Bernard Kouchner voiced his disapproval of the plan, and came to the third Forum to take part in a debate.

In mid-December 2003, the Minister for Health met, each in turn, the main psychoanalytic associations, followed by the psychologists and psychotherapists. The Minister proposed to the psychoanalysts that he withdraw them from the scope of the bill in exchange for the handover of their directories. The directories would be entrusted to the Ministry to check that no unauthorised psychotherapist had slipped in. Putting psychoanalysis under ministerial control, which everyone immediately perceived as the ushering-in of a ministry of the mind, was an unacceptable measure. In the name of the École de la Cause freudienne, its president Lilia Mahjoub refused to go along with this procedure. This was the case for Élisabeth Roudinesco too, who also let it be known that the representatives of the most powerful psychoanalytic societies would, however, be consenting to it. These included:

> The Société psychanalytique de Paris (SPP), the Association psychanalytique de France (APF), both affiliated to the International Psycho-Analytic Association founded in 1910 by Sigmund Freud, along with the Organisation psychanalytique de langue française (OPLF), the Association lacanienne internationale (ALI), and the Société de psychanalyse freudienne (SPF). (Roudinesco, 2004, p. 14, note 1)

In other words, for the first time in France, the state was taking it upon itself to worm its way into a debate between learned societies, even though such action falls entirely outside its jurisdiction. The psychoanalysts of the École de la Cause freudienne refused this slide. Their adversaries, essentially those from the IPA then under the leadership of Daniel Widlöcher, immediately fingered them as the "charlatans" targeted by the Amendment.

> If evidence is needed of this, take the declaration by Bernard Brusset, a member of the SPP. No sooner had the Amendment been passed by the Senate than he rushed, with the complicity of the "good Lacanians" who had rallied to his policy of lists, to pillory the other Lacanians, those from the ECF, accused of imposture for not having respected the "international norms" imposed by the IPA. (Roudinesco, 2004, p. 21)

On that same day, midway through December 2003, the Minister met the psychologists and psychotherapists in the presence of Christian Vasseur and Jean-François Allilaire. Jacques-Alain Miller wondered what significance their presence might hold:

> Who are they? Christian Vasseur, president of the French Psychiatric Association, is Bernard Accoyer's mentor [...] [and he] explains that the "incontrovertible invariants" of psychotherapy are to be found

in medical psychopathology. Allilaire speaks down-the-nose in the Minister's office. He refers to his texts: his white paper,[10] his report for the Académie de médicine, and the Cléry-Melin roadmap too. What does he say? That the Accoyer Amendment is going in the right direction, but that already we should be thinking about drafting the implementing decrees. That the psychotherapists of the future, as well as the future clinical psychologists, will have to be trained in "highly standardised psychotherapies". That this teaching will be taken care of by training institutions, offering programmes "akin to those offered by the Faculty of Medicine". That these institutions will provide training in cognitive-behavioural treatments as well as in psychoanalysis, and even in further specialities, still within a medical framework, or contractualised with psychiatry. That he has major reservations about the approval, stipulated in the Accoyer Amendment, of the "neither-nors" (neither doctor nor psychologist) currently practising. That medicalisation is at any rate unavoidable. (Miller, 2004)

In February 2004, the move to liquidate psychoanalysis saw the opening of a new chapter with a publication from Inserm. Its "assessment" of three types of psychotherapy, one of which was psychoanalysis, concluded by awarding the dunce's cap to the latter. Needless to say, the gold star went to the cognitive-behavioural therapies (CBT). The venerable institution showed no hesitation in passing off the idea that psychoanalysis was merely a branch of medicine and an undeserving one at that. This was made to look like something plain to everyone. Moreover, this *coup de grâce* was dealt shortly after the hostilities began. They were counting on the effect of surprise. What they didn't count on was the wilful courage of a determined few. It had only taken a few months to decipher the situation. Foreseeing the next step would not be impossible. The French department of health, *La Direction générale de la santé* (DGS) had financed the Inserm report. Our research allowed us to anticipate its conclusions. Until then, Inserm had never been contested as a serious institution, and indeed seemed incontestable. Its declaration of war on psychoanalysis was a first. This came as a deep shock not only to the therapists but to the public at large.

In February 2004, William Dab, the director of the DGS, was sufficiently satisfied with the assessment of the psychotherapies for him to hold a press conference on the Inserm premises. The calamitous handling of the previous year's heat wave had hurried on the resignation of Lucien Abenhaïm, and Dab had replaced him at the helm. Trained in Canada, he made no secret of his support for CBT and the biopsychosocial psychiatry he wanted to see develop in France. Listening to him that day I was struck by his determination. One point nevertheless remained obscure. It seemed that, to begin with, the report commissioned by the DGS only concerned CBT. It was in no way a question of comparing CBT and psychoanalysis. How had this report, which was initially dedicated to CBT, all of a sudden become a report that included psychoanalysis, which had never been assessed, contrary to what was being stated? This was not explained.

In Spring 2004, after the regional elections, Philippe Douste-Blazy became Minister of Health. Didier Houssin then took over as head of the DGS. On 20th March 2004, Christian Vasseur organised a debate at Marly-le-Roi under the title *Les Assises de la psychothérapie* [Psychotherapy in the balance].[11] Twenty or so speakers were present, including Allilaire and Brusset, who together drafted a new version of the Amendment.

Chronicle of a defeat foretold

In February 2005, Philippe Douste-Blazy came to the *Forum*. He sided with the psychoanalysis of Freud and Lacan, forswearing the Inserm report. The Minister for Health contested the report's fundamental notion that mental suffering could be evaluated and measured, and promised to have the report taken off the Ministry of Health website. His courageous speech was greeted by a standing ovation. Never before had a publication from Inserm been disowned in this way. It was also true, however, that until then its scientific label had not been up for grabs. We owe it to this enlightened Minister to have forced the Moloch of "psych-" evaluation to back down. It should be added that he had grasped just how dangerous it is to pit one "psych-" profession against another. He was not therefore in any hurry to redraft the implementing decrees for the Accoyer Amendment.

In Spring 2005, the publishing house Navarin brought out *Lacan même* by Philippe Sollers and *Le secret des dieux* by Jacques-Alain Miller. Catherine Clément wrote the French postface, I wrote the preface to the Spanish edition (Miller, 2005a). Seuil published the latest of Lacan's

Seminars to be established by J.-A. Miller, *Le séminaire livre XXIII, Le sinthome*, which went on to become a bestseller.

The reaction was not long coming. After the summer break, the supporters of CBT published the *Livre noir de la psychanalyse*. It needs to be said in no uncertain terms that this tract against psychoanalysis stands as the paradigm of a new revisionism.[12] Bernard-Henri Lévy and Jacques-Alain Miller decided to return fire. They addressed enlightened public opinion with a letter to artists, actors, writers, journalists, poets, politicians, academics, scientists, and psychoanalysts, asking them to speak about what psychoanalysis meant for them, but first and foremost from the position of analysand. It was then decided that the replies would be published as a special feature in Lévy's journal *La règle du jeu*, which he invited me to guest edit. It can be found in Issue 30 which came out in January 2006. A collection of testimonies such as these was unheard of. Usually confined to the pages of our specialist journals, for the first time ever these accounts were being put in the hands of the general public. Sincere, often moving, both dignified and discreet, nearly always brief and to the point, they spelt out, one by one, the truth at stake for each contributor and the *Real* of the affair.

In February 2006, Seuil published the *Anti-livre noir de la psychanalyse* (Miller, 2006b), composed essentially of a series of short and incisive texts presented at the Forum dedicated to CBT, of which it constitutes a careful, documented critique. After the June 2005 European elections, Xavier Bertrand replaced Douste-Blazy at the Ministry for Health. An attentive Minister, he took his bearings from his predecessor. It was no longer possible, however, to postpone the drafting of the implementing decrees for the Accoyer Amendment.

The negotiations and consultations were due to be concluded by the end of 2006. Then, just as the finalised decrees were about to go off to the Council of State, Deputy Accoyer launched a new offensive in Parliament. The transposition of the European directive on medication had been the object of a Bill due to be voted at the National Assembly in February 2007. Accoyer seized on the opportunity of a parliamentary debate on this Bill to submit an Amendment that included two articles regulating the training of psychotherapists. The instigators of the Bill were thus implying that either there were not as yet any decree proposals, or that the decree proposals were too open. The pathology of democracy was rearing its head once more. It was judged unconstitutional. The Council of State quickly abolished these riders, which had been passed by a joint committee, on the grounds that they had nothing to do with medication and constituted what are known as "cavalier articles".

In March 2007, taking up his post as spokesperson for the presidential candidate Nicolas Sarkozy in the run-up to the elections, Xavier Bertrand had to stand down as Minister for Health. Philippe Bas, the incoming Minister, had no time to resolve this delicate problem. It was not until a fifth Minister for Health came in, after election day, that the citizens and their therapists saw their fate sealed. Roselyne Bachelot was the one to inherit this tricky file.

The public benefit of psychoanalysis

During this fight for survival, the École de la Cause freudienne struck a victory that definitively changed the lie of the land. On 5th May 2006, the École was officially recognised by the state as an association in the public interest.[13] A small group of us had spared no effort to secure this formal acknowledgement, as had been Dr Lacan's wish. From now on, his adversaries would not be able to masquerade as the only serious interlocutors with the authorities. This victory did not, however, discourage certain bureaucrats who were hostile to psychoanalysis from launching two further offensives, one after the 2007 summer break, and then another during the summer of 2008.

In Autumn 2007, the Institut National de Prévention et d'Éducation pour la Santé (INPES) launched a campaign on depression in adults, with television and radio adverts, a guide distributed by the thousands, leaflets, and so on. The media supplemented this with interviews, stories, photos, and so forth. But what about the investigations themselves? There were scarcely any, or none at all. This unprecedented all-out publicity campaign had the goal of imposing seven ideas: that depression exists; that it is an illness; that it is spreading in society to the point of being a *recognised public health issue*; that it is therefore to be treated with great urgency; that it can be treated with medication and conditioning; that it has no existential dimension; and that psychoanalysis is not a viable option with which to treat it. Huge amounts of money from the Treasury coffers, along with contributions, at least indirectly, from laboratories, were invested in the unilateral promotion of these seven theses, all of which are highly contestable. Éric Laurent showed that accepting these theses would see us running the risk of taking another step towards the nanny state that seems to be taking shape in the UK (Laurent, É., 2007),[14] where today psychoanalysis is being outlawed.[15]

If, however, there is indeed one public health issue at stake, then it is the prevention of suicides and murder-suicides. They concern adults, but also the youth, and the tendency is present in ever-younger children. How many Virginia Techs and Columbines will it take to grasp that the *passage à l'acte* (whether directed at the self or others) has a logic that psychoanalysis has already brought to light? For Freud, no organic problem can be held responsible for a subject's sadness, only the truth he harbours within him. This is why sadness is often lucid. It is legitimate when there is a bereavement; when it becomes a symptom, however, it remains so for as long as the desire that it encloses is still muzzled. This symptom is necessarily private and intimate, but at the same time it is connected to discontent in society and the latter's prescriptions of unbounded knowledge and power. Thus, to reduce all that is human to a chain of neurones and neurotransmitters is not only to reduce it to servitude, but also to condemn it to permanent depression (Aflalo, 2007).

At the end of June 2008, the leaked draft decree of the Accoyer Amendment sent the troops back into battle. The summer break did not dissuade *Le Nouvel Âne* from putting together (in the space of a month) its ninth issue and from alerting the public in time as to the catastrophic consequences this draft decree could have.[16] Indeed, this version of the decree was putting back on the table the disappearance of psychoanalysis and the totalitarian control of the populace (i.e., two consequences of the Pichot and Allilaire report on the psychotherapies (Pichot & Allilaire, 2003) that had already elicited the enmity of the professionals and general public alike). Once again, bureaucrats were trying to take the reins of power by means of false forms of knowledge that have the look of science. Rejecting the clinic, but hungry for authority, a few psychiatrists did indeed bet on scientism and CBT with an eye to unduly decking themselves out with the "scientific" label (Aflalo, 2008a). Fearful of the liberty and responsibility that science entails, they dreamed of uncovering laws that would control men like machines. In the absence of any such laws, they sent their prayers to the legislators, as though the Republic's laws could take command of the laws of science. They actively sought this as the fate of one and all: their colleagues who refused to bow to their diktat, patients in general, and, little by little, each and every citizen. Meeting up in small circles in different universities, these modern-day incarnations of Thomas Diafoirus decided that the very fact of *speaking* was a medical act that needed to be legislated without further delay. Isn't it about time that *speaking* was recognised as a law of the human species, and its free expression as the fundament of our democracy?

The knowledge devised by these experts, set out in psychiatric handbooks like the *Diagnostic and Statistical Manual of Mental Disorders*, produces more victims every day. After years of purges and cuts, the profession is stricken, the patients misunderstood, and the public needlessly endangered. The new profession of psychotherapist invented by the draft decree stems from a fierce eagerness to regulate the speech that is exchanged between two persons, and to use state power to impose silence on those who suffer. As long as psycho/psychiatric scientism goes on spreading its wrongdoing, the number of victims will go on rising. The time has come to recognise that our duty to these victims is at one with the preventive step that entails analysing the discontent in civilisation. Were the "psych-" professions to refuse to put up a fight, they would meet defeat and dishonour far in excess of their strict professional exercise. Putting oneself in the service of the victims requires that we see, as did Baltasar Gracián, that a world of prejudice has to be overturned: a world in which "virtue is persecuted, and vice applauded, truth silenced, and falsity endued with a threefold tongue."[17] This question is crucial.

Happiness: a new idea in "mental healthcare"

In early March 2009, a new Amendment replaced the Accoyer Bill. Madame Roselyne Bachelot, then Minister for Health,[18] herself defended it before the National Assembly who passed it unanimously. We may be grateful to the elected representatives for having grasped the importance of this Bill and for having expressed as much in their vote. We should also praise the courage and determination of Madame Bachelot.[19] But we know too that this step forward will not really have been taken until the implementing decrees that are still being drawn up have confirmed it. It is reasonable to assume that their imminent publication in the *Journal officiel de la République française*, the official gazette of the French Republic, will stave off for a while the rear-guard action against psychoanalysis that I have just outlined.

As for the *Failed Assassination of Psychoanalysis*, it came to an end soon after the publication of the Inserm report. Over six months or so, from October 2003 to April 2004, it would not have taken much for psychoanalysis to fall under the yoke of a clique of academics who had propelled themselves into the corridors of power. They had managed to convince the nation's representatives of their attachment to the *Res publica*. Then, the smattering of deputies from the left and right who were present during the first reading in the National Assembly voted in favour of the Accoyer Amendment. So it was that they unwittingly opened the hunt for "charlatans"—which amounted to a witch-hunt for Lacanian psychoanalysts (clearly the ones being targeted by the instigators of this Bill). Factors such as the length of the sessions and the training of psychoanalysts were already crystallising fierce opposition to Lacan's teaching during his lifetime, but it was after his death in 1981 that his detractors, for the most part Parisians, took up their fight against his teaching. While they laboured away at wiping out Lacan's teaching, Jacques-Alain Miller was working to build an international association worthy of housing it: the World Association of Psychoanalysis (WAP).

In the meantime, "happiness" became one of the stakes in public health policy. It came on the scene with the odd idea that there exists a "mental health" that may be conceived of and defined as a "scientifically" measurable state of happiness. Yet, if we take into account the difficulty of achieving such a state, whether temporarily or permanently, this amounted to declaring the whole of humanity "mentally ill". After the commodification of the body—which had been under way for some time—it was now the turn of the soul. Humanity had just sold its soul to the occult powers of an academic psychiatry won over to "shrink-commerce" and utterly determined to bring down psychoanalysis, which in their eyes was the guilty party on account of favouring each subject one-by-one over wide-scale, high-yield calculations.

The improbable then became possible. It took the form of a piece of legislation on the psychotherapies that embraced this idea of happiness. It was not about a *right to happiness*—this is not the United States[20]—but the therapists' *duty* to ensure the happiness of citizens. By making their ideology pass for a "science", and in managing to get it legalised, this university clique finally had in its grasp the means to gain the power it had coveted for so long and to force the Lacanian psychoanalysts to capitulate on Lacan's teaching. By compelling all mental health professionals to adopt the standardised methods in force in the IPA, the bill would prohibit a scientific debate—a crucial debate—on the length of sessions and the training of psychoanalysts. This debate had been opened by Freud himself, and was pursued by Lacan. Now it looked like it was going to be declared obsolete. From now on, only the protocol and other formalities of evaluation that had been devised in the said universities would come stamped with the "science" label and be authorised as such. Therefore, they saw winning the battle of the implementing decrees as a critical step. This was just what it would take to win the lucrative monopoly on the university training of therapists.

That was so, but psychoanalysis is an experience of the subject, and without freedom, the subject's responsibility cannot be engaged. This means that psychoanalysis cannot be practised outside of a space of liberty which only democracy can guarantee. In casting aside the principles of liberty with an eye to breaching psychoanalysis, Lacan's enemies also showed themselves to be enemies of the Enlightenment and the values of the French Republic.

Readings

For supporters of cognitive-behavioural therapy, the lists of questions it employs have been decreed "tools of scientific measure". They are the key to the success of the knowledge in contemporary psychiatry. In France, Jean Cottraux's publications give some idea of this. In one of his books, we read:

> Works of psychopathology [...] endeavour to answer [...] the questions posed by clinical practice, questions which are destined for more or less immediate practical application. We are finally catching up with other developed countries that have long been creating a space for biopsychosocial research. (Cottraux & Bouvard, 2005, p. 1)

The watchword "psychopathology", to which Freud made us prick up our ears, is actually on this occasion being borrowed from Daniel Widlöcher. The "psychopathology" signifier is what makes the principles of Cottraux's book legible for us: firstly, to support, as does Widlöcher, the ideology of biopsychosocial psychiatry, and secondly, to approve the connection between CBT and Widlöchian psychoanalysis.

Epidemiology in mental healthcare is a newcomer in the field of psychiatry. In this, we may observe the neo-hygienist slide of biopsychosocial psychiatry. In conformity with the ideas of CBT, the psychoanalytic and psychiatric clinic is being emptied of its content and replaced by a practice of questionnaires. These methods have been contributing to the spread of a dubious ideology that underpins a new radicalism. In France, Dr Viviane Kovess is a specialist in "mental health" epidemiology. With Dr Pascal, she co-authored the "Cléry-Melin report". In her publications, Pascal and Cléry-Melin are cited in the references. As for Widlöcher, who wrote the preface to her book on epidemiology and mental health, his name features heavily in the bibliography.

Another book, the 1980 publication *Psychiatrie clinique: Une approche biopsychosociale* (Lalonde, Aubut, & Grunberg, 1999), comes to us from Canada. The French healthcare authorities are seeking to implant the ideas outlined therein in France, despite the catastrophic consequences they have had in North America. Biopsychosocial psychiatry is passing itself off as a scientific humanism when it is actually more akin to a kind of bioreligion in the service of a CBT that aims to wipe psychoanalysis off the map. Widlöcher and Allilaire's treatise on psychopathology took up these same theses some fifteen years down the line (Widlöcher, 1994).

As to the more or less immediate consequences of these theses, the Inserm report published at the end of February 2004 showed what they were made of. The results of the assessment of three forms of psychotherapy, including CBT and psychoanalysis, were quite predictable: all the experts consulted for the finalisation of the report were favourable to CBT. This was especially the case for Widlöcher. This publication stands as the fermata to a score orchestrated by "scientific" psychiatry. Its designs on "mental health" marketing are more clearly visible, and are very much part of the failed assassination attempt on psychoanalysis that was supposed to usher in the Orwellian project of the annexation of civil liberties.

It was time to face up to facts. All my different readings were converging towards the same point on the horizon: the various publications of Daniel Widlöcher. His *Traité de psychopathologie* duplicated the theses of French Canadian psychiatry and "mental health" epidemiology. It was drafted in collaboration with colleagues of his who have since come out in favour of the Accoyer Amendment. Widlöcher also drafted two sections of the White Paper for psychiatry. Moreover, just like Cottraux, Widlöcher is an honorary member of a CBT association. Over Easter 2004, I set about reading his available publications. The telltale thread that ran through each of these texts—what in psychoanalysis we would call their "quilting point"—was a move to forcibly cognitivise Freudian psychoanalysis that reached right back to the 1980s. These publications were clearly motivated by a will to ensure that nothing would remain of the teaching of Freud and Lacan. Chapters Two and Three of this book are thus dedicated to a commentary on some of Widlöcher's key ideas. The last chapter tries to shed light on some of the particularities of the Zeitgeist that made the failed assassination attempt on psychoanalysis possible.

I must say that to read this psychiatric literature was not my first instinct. There could be no doubt, however, as to its strong implication in our present-day situation once one publication after the next served only to confirm the roles and identities of the main players behind the event. From the *instant of seeing* at the end of October 2003 to the *moment to conclude* at the start of January 2004, two full months went by, during which time I took on board Jacques-Alain Miller's initial request. Lacan asked of the psychoanalysts of his School that they ensure an ongoing commentary on the analytic movement, together with census reports on publications related to psychoanalysis, particularly those from psychiatry. Today we have to admit that we fell short on this point.

At the end of October 2003, just after the first reading of the Accoyer Amendment, the École de la Cause freudienne held its study days at the Palais des congrès in Paris. When I heard Jacques-Alain Miller speak at the event, his carefully measured words resounded like a tocsin. Mobilisation was already under way by the early hours of the next morning. I sought the help of a few close associates, in particular my journalist colleagues. Miller quickly alerted the public at large (Miller, 2005b). He was invited to speak on different radio stations and television channels. The political journalist Jean-Pierre Elkabbach was the first to interview him for Public Sénat and Europe 1. By the end of November, Miller had launched the journal *Le Nouvel Âne* and I agreed to join him as assistant director. While we were working together on this magazine, he asked me to read the literature that had given rise to the offensive. I did the rounds of several medical and general bookshops in Paris and acquired a number of books. Reading this literature over the winter break helped me to decipher the situation we were going through. From January to February 2004, I wrote four articles on "Cognitive-behavioural therapy", "Epidemiology in mental healthcare", "Biopsychosocial psychiatry", and "The Inserm report". The first three correspond, in re-written form, to Chapters Four and Six of this book. The last appears as Appendix II.

The battle is just beginning, and it will be long-drawn-out. But this is the price to pay for *La gaia scienza*.

CHAPTER TWO

Procrustes and the river of sludge I

> Moved by an extreme mistrust of the power of human wishes [...] [psychoanalysts] are ready for the sake of attaining some fragment of objective certainty, to sacrifice everything. [...] They will be ready to employ the methods of scientific enquiry only as a ladder to raise them over the head of science. Heaven help us if they climb to such a height!
>
> —S. Freud, *"Psychoanalysis and telepathy"*

The "psychoanalysis of the future"

The various publications authored by the psychoanalyst Daniel Widlöcher can teach us many valuable lessons. In 2001, he was president of the International Psycho-Analytic Association (IPA) founded by Freud. Back at the start of the 1980s, Widlöcher was already airing his concern for the future of psychoanalysis, but it was in 1996 that he thought he had identified the three main threats that hung over it and the remedies that would save it. Analytic treatment is purportedly being progressively abandoned in favour of the psychotherapies, for the reason that the public, according to Widlöcher, deem the latter to be faster and better value for money. He considers, therefore, that loss of public interest and the risk of dilution represent two significant dangers that lie in wait for psychoanalysis (Widlöcher, 1996, pp. 47–68). But he is above all preoccupied by what he calls its "risk of implosion". He imputes this risk to "charismatic personalities like Lacan". Widlöcher's remedy was quite simple: psychoanalysis needs more science, more laws, and less Lacanian practice.

Medicalising psychoanalysis

Widlöcher considers that to move forward with success into the twenty-first century, psychoanalysis must become a medical science. This temptation is not a new one. Freud fought it energetically because he saw that the psychical symptoms to which psychoanalysis tends are linked to language and not to the organism. Indeed, this is the very crux of Freud's discovery. It was the reason why the affected bodies of hysterics led him to usher in psychoanalysis and not some new branch of medicine. It was also why he came down on the side of the non-medical practice of psychoanalysis. He explained himself on this matter on several occasions, in particular in "The question of lay analysis" (Freud, 1926e).

The North American psychoanalysts have always refused to take on board the autonomy of the psychoanalyst with respect to medicine. For a long time they refused to accord the title "psychoanalyst" to those analysands who had ended their analyses and who were judged to have completed their training satisfactorily, but who were not qualified doctors. Some years ago, they were officially reprehended, and, it has to be said, each time they were taken to court by these non-doctor analysands who found themselves being denied the title they were seeking, they lost the case. Freud's idea was that to become a psychoanalyst, it would be better to be erudite. But he also considered that the necessary condition of this practice lies in the fact of having gone through one's own analysis. Thus, the discriminatory argument of university qualification does not hold water when it comes to qualifying oneself as a psychoanalyst. Lacan took the same line as Freud in this debate, for the same reasons.

It is clear that the bone of contention that is still dividing psychoanalysts today is the training of psychoanalysts. There are those who, like Freud and Lacan, acknowledge the utterly unprecedented character of the analytic discourse and judge it necessary to draw the right conclusions when it comes to defining analysts' training. Then there are those against whom Freud and Lacan fought relentlessly because they refused this unprecedented character and its consequences. They seek rather to fold it back onto the university discourse. Examining a few psychoanalytic concepts will show the antinomy of these two discourses, but one example can offer us an immediate insight into what is at stake.

To make a symptom yield, the psychoanalyst must find its cause, because the subject who comes to speak to him is unaware of what makes him suffer. After the preliminary interviews, the analyst asks his patient to lie down on the couch and to say what comes to him in the form it comes to him. In other words, he asks him to respect the rule of free association. If the patient is ignorant of what is producing his malaise, how would the analyst be able to know it for him? On the other hand, the psychoanalyst knows that everything the subject is going to say must be retained so as to identify the cause of what is wrong, which the subject speaks about without realising. To put it another way, the analyst's knowledge is simply *supposed* knowledge. There is nothing of the like in medicine.

When a patient consults a doctor because his leg is broken, clearly the doctor does not ask him to voice the ideas this event calls to mind. He makes a clinical examination, then sends him for an x-ray so as to establish the diagnosis and prescribe the right treatment. He goes about things in this way because the knowledge required for the practice of medicine is an objective knowledge that is valid for anybody and everybody. Meanwhile, the supposed knowledge of the psychoanalyst is singular. Though the psychoanalyst knows nothing of the analysand who comes to consult him, the analysand nevertheless attributes knowledge to him regarding the cause of his discontent. Unconscious as it is, the knowledge extracted from the analytic experience is constructed in the time of the analytic session itself. This knowledge is only valid for this one particular analysand, and thus cannot be generalised into university teaching. Moreover, analysis is an experience of the lifting of repression, which reconciles the subject with the values that count most for him. It is therefore an experience that modifies the subject. The university awards qualifications; it does not offer subjective experiences such as these. This is why it is not wrong to consider the choice of psychoanalyst as invariably entailing a share of risk, regardless of his qualifications. This risk nevertheless remains limited when you ask the opinion of a close one or contact a school of psychoanalysis.

The idea of a diploma that would be valid as a guarantee of "good practice" in psychoanalysis is utterly foreign to the psychoanalysis of Freud and Lacan. We can ask ourselves, therefore, whether this idea does not aim at the disappearance of the Freudian discipline as such, in its very principle. Isn't this an expression of the same will to wipe out the analytic discourse that has been present in one form or another since its emergence at the dawn of the twentieth century?

Widlöcher justifies the resurgence of this lost cause as a means to bring about the "scientifisation" of psychoanalysis by means of the advances in neuroscience and the contributions of cognitive science. These two disciplines are quite foreign to psychoanalysis and bear no relation to it. As for the arguments employed to convince us of the legitimacy of this enterprise, they amount to a collection of outlandish ideas inherited from the scientism of CBT. We are going to be analysing these arguments in detail. We can, however, already grasp how the *medicalisation* of psychoanalysis is being made to serve as a guarantee for the public. Once decked out with the "scientific" label, psychoanalysis would ostensibly be more serious and more presentable (Widlöcher, 1996, p. 69).

Yet, though it operates on the edge of science, psychoanalysis is neither a medical discipline nor a science. For Freud and Lacan alike, psychoanalysis is unthinkable without scientific rigour. But the Real it grapples with is the Real of the subject's jouissance.[1] The subject can grasp a logical part of this Real, but his jouissance can be neither spoken nor written, and thus it can be neither objectified nor measured. So, in an attempt to circumvent this obstacle, in the hope of claiming to reach a scrap of certitude, the Freudian discipline is being sacrificed on the altar of evaluation that we owe to cognitive-behavioural scientism.

The imposture of evaluation

The evaluation in question here has nothing to do with the methodology used by epistemologists (Milner, 2005b, p. 10)[2]. The practices involved here come from product monitoring procedures in the car industry. In the industrial sector, a series of check sheets is useful for the quality control of engine manufacture. Once established by means of rated scales, the quality of the engine is subjected to statistical calculations which are then logged in its "health record". The advocates of CBT have taken up this industrial method and applied it to their patients' minds. They came up with the idea of establishing a "mental health record" by applying this technique to the control of humans. The culture of evaluation has not spread to this field alone; all sectors of our modern democracies have been progressively affected by it to the point that today it is reigning supreme. Under the cover of abiding by budgetary constraints, it means to govern humans as though they were industrial products. A minority of academics won over by CBT have been presenting this method as a science, when in fact it is merely a Kafkaesque bureaucratic discourse that seeks to control everything without ever being controlled itself (*cf*. Miller & Milner, 2004).

Evaluation is one of the names of our contemporary discontent. So how then is it to be explained that the former president of the International Association founded by Freud should decide to compound the discontent in civilisation instead of analysing it? Why opt for a variation of psychoanalysis that is in thrall to a false science? One can't help noticing that the triumph of evaluation would effectively guarantee for these academics control over the training of psychologists at the university. Furthermore, and this is not the least of it, were they to become the masters of the practice of each and every psychoanalyst, they might succeed in liquidating Lacanianism. In their minds, the danger we all need to avoid is a mystery to no one, it has been clearly identified and named: "Lacanian charlatanism".

Legalising the unconscious

The appeal to the legislator becomes clearer when considered in the light of Lacan's excommunication from the IPA forty years ago.[3] Today, they have set themselves the task of gaining political power so as to legitimise by law that which the force of the IPA ban did not manage to secure in the early 1960s: to silence Lacan's discourse and deny him his status as a psychoanalyst. It would thereby be possible to be rid of his teaching—in France if not across the world—along with those who today still adhere to this teaching.

It is by no means certain that the exercise of democracy is compatible with this call upon legislators to intervene in a debate of ideas between learned associations. Furthermore, this is surely why they tried to make the legislators believe that in laying down the law they would be acting for the good of psychoanalysis. They tried to convince the politicians that in this way the implosion of psychoanalysis would be avoided, decreeing Lacanian practices to be unlawful on the grounds that they are "lighter", with fewer sessions per week, shorter sessions, less interpretation, and so on (Widlöcher, 1996, p. 18).

Needless to say, it would be way off the mark to reckon the Lacanian orientation to be "lighter", since what defines it is its orientation towards the Real. On the other hand, one of the mainstreams in the IPA—an academic and essentially North American current—decided to reject the Real of the subject's jouissance so as to be able to cognitivise psychoanalysis and thereby make it compatible with *marketable* knowledge. It is this current of the IPA that is represented in France by Widlöcher. The grotesque idea of a legalised unconscious might raise a smile, but obtaining more science, more legislation, and less Lacanian practice for psychoanalysis, describes the make-up of the very programme that threw the French therapeutic world into turmoil and triggered the events of 2003–2004. There can be no doubt that the sizeable and immediate mobilisation of numerous intellectuals and pre-eminent personalities standing shoulder to shoulder with the analysts staved off the imminence of the peril, but the fight was not over.

Extinction on the agenda

Beyond the scientistic offensive in France, the discontent induced by advances in science has left its mark on our civilisation. Masters have always wanted things to run smoothly without symptoms coming along to block their path. Today, the master is demanding the widespread implementation of evaluation; evaluation that is set to run with scientific efficacy because it promises to get to the bottom of all that does not run smoothly. Evaluation becomes scientism when its object is a living and speaking object. It is already difficult to concede that the quality of an object can be evaluated scientifically, so how can one entertain this for a subject? When applied to all that is human, evaluation covers its ears to the impasses of our civilisation and in so doing reinforces them. One simple question emerges in this regard: will the Real of jouissance at issue in psychoanalysis continue to insist and produce symptoms, or will it soon be absorbed back into science and the scientism that always comes with it? The responsibility of psychoanalysts is part and parcel of this debate.

The discourse of science can be reproached for its futility because it cannot treat the Real of jouissance that affects us, one and all, and which is sometimes felt as a discontent that is hard to express. Today, however, the danger of a psychoanalysis that has surrendered to its "scientificity" is not simply its futility, it is first and foremost the danger of its very extinction. Widlöcher's publications fulfil this agenda. Since the Freudian discipline is recalcitrant to the measures of man that Widlöcher means to impose, he has made it lie down on a Procrustean bed. Then, adjusting the ends to the means, he clips and trims its fundamental concepts one after the next, making them fit one self-same entity: Widlöcherian thought. The unconscious becomes "thought"; so too desire; and likewise for the drive, anxiety, the affects, transference, interpretation, and so forth. Everything becomes *thought*.

The unconscious and desire

Blending Brentano, hermeneutics, and neuroscience, Widlöcher's philosophical conceptions forge a new vision of humankind, one that is devoid of all substance. As for the Freudian discovery, it was carried off into the fields of the natural sciences, then liquidated, leaving no further obstacles to the advent of the totalitarian regime of "scientific psychology". To establish this agenda, Widlöcher takes up the arguments of CBT's adherents, and first of all their question: "How are the unconscious and desire to be assimilated?" (Widlöcher, 1996, p. 72).

Cognitivising Brentano

Brentano, whose lessons Freud attended, denied the existence of nonconscious psychical phenomena. His work comes as a godsend, therefore, to those who harbour the plan of doing away with the Freudian unconscious by trimming it down to fit CBT and dressing it up from head to toe in new clothes (Widlöcher, 1996, pp. 69–95). We can thus grasp how *psychology from the empirical viewpoint* might whet the appetite of any would-be predator who would appropriate it without regard for the finer points of phenomenology that Husserl for one examined.

In any speech-based treatment, there occurs nothing but an exchange of words. For Widlöcher the positivist, however, the positive and observable fact of the session is not an exchange of words but an exchange of thoughts.[4] The idea that thoughts would be directly accessible to the other party without going via speech can be found in the clinical entities of paranoia and obsessional neurosis. In the first case it is an unshakable certainty, in the second, a fantasy. The Rat Man is the first obsessional patient whose case Freud published. The Rat Man would sometimes be consumed by the idea that other people had access to his thoughts, but he was forced to admit that he must have spoken them aloud without realising. Regardless of whether it is a scientific delusion or a scientistic fantasy, needs must face facts: the patient's thoughts elude any objective observation.

Widlöcher asserts, however, that the unconscious is made up of observable thoughts that precede their uttering, as though one might grasp the thoughts wordlessly. Back in his 1986 *Métapsychologie du sens*, he asserts that *in the beginning was action*, and not "the word". His way of dismissing the function of speech and the field of language presents the dual incentive of rejecting in one fell swoop both the Freudian discovery and Lacan's teaching with its axiom: *the unconscious is structured like a language*. Thereafter it is easier to do away with the Freudian hypothesis of the unconscious. One has only to adopt the idea that the CBT adherents have of the unconscious, namely, that it is the contrary of consciousness: a pre-existent knowledge waiting to be discovered. Next, our positivist declares thought and action to be identical. Surely all this amounts to a misreading of the clinical fact of procrastination, inhibited action, and delaying, when the subject is overwhelmed by his thoughts? Might this fact have escaped Widlöcher's notice despite being well documented by the finest writers of antiquity, and, more recently, by psychoanalysts?

Widlöcher further postulates that thoughts command actions, and that thoughts are intentional actions. The reference to Brentano's notion of intentional action is supposed to justify the outlandish concoction of the Widlöchian unconscious and resolve the delicate problem of the negativity of desire. For Brentano, to desire is to desire something as an object, but only in consciousness, for as we have seen, Brentano rejects any idea of an unconscious. Neglecting this detail, Widlöcher postulates that desire and thought are one and the same. Carved up in this way, the unconscious and desire would become observable thoughts that owe nothing to speech and language. Doesn't this contradict once more the self-evident fact that words stumble, and sometimes even move faster than thoughts? Moreover, if one dispenses with speech and language, how is one to account for the transmission of thoughts without sliding into the rut of telepathy which is scarcely compatible with science? These facts leave the impartial observer pondering. How, then, in all seriousness, is this patchwork to be deemed to have anything to do with the observation of an analysand addressing an analyst?

The subject of science

Materialist and reductionist theories of the mind reject body/soul duality. Indeed, they suppose that everything that goes to make up humankind can be boiled down to matter, to the human organism, and that we may thereby come to know everything about the human mind. Treating the inaugural step of modern science with disdain, they reject the subject of the *cogito*. The "scientific" psychology that is a by-product of these conceptions does not distinguish between human and animal. Yet, by virtue of the fact that the human being speaks, he is quite distinct from the creatures of the animal kingdom. It didn't take psychoanalysis to teach us this, but psychoanalysis operates through speech and speech is its necessary condition. It is built upon this specific distinction that is unique to humankind and it teaches us that, in speaking, the human being is exiled from any direct relationship with nature. Denying this difference between man and animal amounts to negating the very possibility of psychoanalysis.

"Scientific" psychology objectifies what is human: it defines what is human and treats it as an object. To objectify the human being is clearly to deny him the status of subject. More to the point, it is to refuse him his status as a speaking, desiring subject, and in particular his status as a subject responsible for his jouissance. "Scientific" psychology rejects the subject because it is only at this high price that it can assert that the psyche obeys the laws of science, as does the organism, and that it is strictly determined, regardless of what one might say about it.

The Freudian discipline is incompatible with this postulate (and in this respect it sides with religion and the major schools of philosophy, albeit for different reasons) because the subject cannot be eliminated from the analytic experience. For Freud, the subject presents at least two characteristics: he manifests himself in an evanescent way in the language of the formations of the unconscious; and he bears the stamp of division (*Ich-Spaltung*). Lacan links these two characteristics by showing that it is language that divides the subject. Next, he demonstrates how this division allows for the subject of psychoanalysis to be identified with the subject of science, since the Freudian concept of the subject bears the structure of the subject of the Cartesian *cogito*.

Furthermore, in Lacan's teaching, the subject's division is the other name for desire, and desire is always articulated to jouissance. Lacan was already outlining these constructions back in his seventh seminar on *The Ethics of Psychoanalysis* (Lacan, 1992). How can one possibly comprehend Kant's moral law (which opens onto an ethics) without making room for a responsible subject? This responsible subject is a desiring subject who grapples with jouissance. Contrary to Descartes, to Kant, to Freud, and to Lacan, Widlöcher's "science" rejects the subject and claims to be able to do without him while still knowing his thoughts. Thus he asserts that the question of the subject "has no meaning for a psychoanalyst" (Widlöcher, 2003, p. 209).

The method

It is true that the rejection of the subject is necessary for "scientific" psychology, following as it does the positivist epistemology of Auguste Comte and seeking to apply Claude Bernard's experimental method to mankind. This empirical method assures us that everything may be seen and known about the human being, who is no different from an animal or a thing. It claims to be based solely on positive, observable and objective facts. Once these facts have been isolated, they are analysed to extract the scientific laws that govern them.

What was Freud's position regarding the description of the phenomena of analytic experience? In his metapsychological papers, he noted the following:

> Even when simply describing the material, we cannot avoid applying to it certain abstract ideas, acquired from somewhere or other but certainly not just from the new observations alone. (Freud, 2005a, p. 13)

Indeed, when one tries to define the psyche, the fiction that "everything is observable and directly accessible" no longer holds water. Any claim to the contrary cannot help but fall under the heading of scientism. The idea that what is human can be seen and known in its entirety is a fantasy, of which Bentham's Panopticon stands as a striking example.

The hypothesis of the Freudian unconscious

Freud's judgement on experimental method is not contingent; it is a structural necessity demonstrated by his definition and employment of the fundamental concepts of psychoanalysis. The unconscious is one of these concepts. For Freud, the unconscious is not an observable fact, it is a necessary hypothesis when it comes to accounting for a series of facts that includes parapraxes (such as slips of the tongue and bungled actions), witticisms, and dreams, but also symptoms; in a word, everything that Freud designated as "formations of the unconscious". Freud's first three books are devoted to these formations and together constitute the birth certificate of psychoanalysis (Freud, 1900a, 1901b, 1905c). In them, he shows how these manifestations of the unconscious are endowed with signification, even though they seem to be bereft of any. He specifies that this signification manifests itself, unbeknownst to the subject, because it is encoded in two rhetorical figures that encipher its manifestation: *Verdichtung* (condensation) and *Verschiebung* (displacement).

Lacan in turn showed how the formations of the unconscious are messages. This is what led him to say that Freud anticipated the discoveries of Ferdinand de Saussure and Roman Jakobson with respect to the signifier and the signified, and metaphor and metonymy (*cf*. Aflalo, 2004b). When Lacan posits that *the unconscious is structured like a language*, he is doing little more than teasing out the logical consequences of Freud's discoveries. The hypothesis of the unconscious finds its logical structure with Lacan. In the analytic experience, everything happens as though there were a pre-existent knowledge, a knowledge that operates under wraps, unbeknownst to the subject. The Lacanian concept of the *subject supposed to know*, which we mentioned above, accounts for this odd knowledge. It is elaborated in the subject's speech over the course of the sessions if, and only if, the psychoanalyst responds to the subject in the right way. Through a retroactive effect, the knowledge appears to be "already there". The formations of the unconscious cannot be objectified, but they can be subjectified, and they need to be. They fall within the function of speech, the field of language, and the instance of the letter: *culture*, therefore, and not *nature*. This means that Widlöcher's eagerness to *naturalise* the unconscious necessarily entails renouncing Freud's discovery.

The negativity of desire

The concept of desire is a further objection to psychoanalysis being absorbed back into a pseudo-scientific materialist empiricism. In the analytic experience, desire manifests itself as an indestructible negativity because it is conditioned by an object that is lost forever, one that no other object can adequately replace. Freud formalised this lost object in his 1905 *Three Essays on the Theory of Sexuality* (1905d), but Socrates can already be heard explaining it in the *Symposium* based on what he had garnered from Diotima. In *Seminar X*, Lacan conceptualises the condition of desire, which he names "object cause of desire", and also "object *a*" (Lacan, 2014b). So, once again it is impossible to naturalise and positivise desire without losing it *ipso facto*. To the question "how does one naturalise the unconscious and desire?", we reply, therefore, that such an undertaking is impossible if they are not to be irremediably lost. Neither the unconscious nor desire is a positive fact: the unconscious is but a hypothesis, and desire a negativity.

"Hermeneutics"

Widlöcher tailors a hermeneutic outfit for psychoanalysis, one that is unencumbered by linguistics. Meaning is no longer a matter of semantics, but what he calls "thought-action". In the Widlöchian lexicon, giving an account of the "non-conscious" means giving sense to "thought-action". This is why, going against Freud and the very experience of psychoanalysis, this former president of the Freudian International asserts that just because dreams have meaning, this does not mean that they are a language (Widlöcher, 1986, p. 33). Let's say it again: for Widlöcher, the unconscious is nothing more than *what has not yet become conscious*. One would be hard pushed to flatten out Freud's discovery any further than that. Moreover, this "science" does not tell us how to resolve the thorny problem of the objective observation of dreams which have to be grasped in their actuality as observable facts. Would the analysand have to sleep during his sessions? And if he does not talk in his sleep, how are his thoughts to be transmitted to the listener?

Remember that for Freud the important thing was not so much the fact of the dream as putting it into words during the session. Thus, for example, those moments when doubt surfaces as the dream is being recounted were for him a precious colophon indicative of the presence of the desiring subject. Furthermore, Freud considered the analysis of the dream to be unending, since the navel of the dream always preserves an unanalysable portion of non-meaning. Widlöchian hermeneutics on the other hand no longer leaves any room for non-meaning.

"Neurological sciences"

If it were to scale the divine ladder of science, psychoanalysis would still have to conform to the measuring rod of the natural sciences. The neurosciences serve as an alibi here, imposing the idea of equivalence between brain and thought, between the state of cerebral matter and the activity of thinking (Widlöcher, 1986, p. 50). This idea, which falls in line with the habit of renaming everything "thought", is foreign to science as well. So, Widlöcher the incorrigible materialist delves into the cognitive-behavioural prop cupboard. Rallying to the CBT cause, he hoists up their flag to let it flap in the winds that whistle through the university, a flag that shimmers in the golden light of the dream of human subjugation, for the thoughts of man so enslaved (set as they are by hereditary genetic programmes) clear him of any responsibility. Can one in all seriousness imagine that MRI intracranial neuronal activity flashing up on a display panel will allow us to say anything whatsoever about thoughts themselves?

The subject who is thereby mistaken for the folds in his brain begets some very peculiar desiring objects. Does the idea that an organ, even a cerebral one, is able to desire, belong to science? Doesn't it stem, rather, from a misguided psychology that entertains belief in a neuronal man? Need we call to mind that the ethics of psychoanalysis brooks no evasive loophole? Since Freud, the empire of responsibility has extended up to and including the unconscious itself.

Outstripping Freud

Needless to say, this would-be return to a pre-Freudian unconscious aims to wipe out the Freudian invention. Widlöcher would like to replace it with CBT, and this is why he is seeking to recast Freud not as the discoverer of the unconscious and the inventor of psychoanalysis, but as the precursor of CBT (Widlöcher, 2003, especially p. 17 & p. 138).

The first and second generation Freudians of the IPA moved away from Freud, deeming him old hat. Some of them promoted a "post-Freud" in the same vein as Ego Psychology. Their failure led ensuing generations to strive to show how Freud was out of touch, jumping back to a "pre-Freud". Today they are trying to make us believe that he discovered neither the unconscious nor desire, nor even did he invent psychoanalysis. Each time their goal is the same: to absorb psychoanalysis back into psychology. This is why Lacan never stopped fighting the obscurantism of the psychologising tendency in the IPA (*cf.* Lacan, 2014a), and why today the resources of his teaching are allowing us to go on fighting the obscurantism that is plaguing the psychoanalysis that Freud invented over a century ago.

The structure of language proper to the unconscious is the very essence of the Freudian discovery. For psychoanalysis, the unconscious has no other Being besides speech, language, and their effects, and this is why the unconscious is *ethical* and not *ontic*. Rejecting this fact constitutes a foreclosure of the symbolic.

With the ethics of psychoanalysis

To summarise what we have seen: first of all, psychoanalysis cannot be absorbed into science, and empirical method does not suit it, for concept precedes precept. Indeed, the concept is what allows practice to be ordered, it does not emerge from it. Therefore, it is not apposite to assert that Freud was a positivist.

Next, the Freudian discipline is not a hermeneutics because it preserves the necessary place of non-meaning. The experience of psychoanalysis consists in ascertaining those watchwords that are loaded with the weight of libido and which turn the subject's life into a destiny. Once the symptom has delivered the different metaphorical meanings of these words, the point of non-meaning is reached and the *master signifiers* are deactivated. The analytic experience can unravel this destiny, and thus it is not a fate pre-inscribed in one's genes. One can say that hermeneutics is a modality of *enjoy-meant* of the signifier, but it is neither a mode of its observation nor its extraction.

Thirdly, to define desire with reference to the desired object is to turn one's back on the indestructible negativity of Freudian desire. It is also to reject the object cause of desire conceptualised by Lacan. The teleological conception of desire that limits it to its finality thereby rejects its cause. Thus, defining desire as a thought-act fails to recognise the structural negativity of desire and brings about the foreclosure of the object that causes it.

Lastly, the (Freudian or Lacanian) unconscious is articulated with desire and jouissance, and it accords the subject his place. The "scientific psychoanalysis" that Widlöcher advocates has rejected both in one fell swoop. But our Procrustes has not stopped there. Bit by bit, he has gone on to give the Freudian concepts of anxiety and the drive a makeover, defining as he does so what he believes analytic practice should be.

CHAPTER THREE

Procrustes and the river of sludge II

Scientism is not a new phenomenon. As we have seen, it follows science like a shadow, spreading its harmful effects in its name. This is how it has come to cling to psychoanalysis since its inception. Freud, Lacan, and all psychoanalysts worthy of the name, have had to fight it relentlessly. Of course, it is in the name of science that Daniel Widlöcher claims to revisit the Freudian corpus. If the university current of the IPA to which he belongs is to be taken seriously, it is because it is incidental to a phenomenon that is specific to our scientific and utilitarian civilisation. At a time when physical and "mental" health is the main stake in a profit-driven market economy, we may safely predict that the legislation offensive will not be limited to a few countries in Europe. Holding out against this utilitarian ogre is going to be a critical step.

Widlöcher's revision has subsumed a good many of the fundamental concepts of psychoanalysis, as we have shown. The concept of the drive is targeted in particular. Indeed, Freud forged this concept in order to restore jouissance (which science rejects, and which comes back with much greater force in the psychical symptom) to its proper place.

The drive

Widlöcher makes no secret of his decision to do away with the concept of the drive (Widlöcher, 1996, pp. 69–96; Widlöcher, 2003, p. 302). Once it has likewise been transformed into "thought", the Freudian discovery is corseted into the "scientific" uniform of CBT. The clothes don't make the man. Could they possibly make a science?

Jouissance

We have seen that formations of the unconscious are endowed with signification even when they seem to be devoid of any. Freud further shows that this signification is linked to a satisfaction of which the subject is oblivious. The case of one of his patients, the Rat Man, shows this clearly. As he was telling Freud about the "rat torture" at the root of his obsession, the young man allowed his face to reflect the horror of a jouissance, a jouissance that was his, but "of which he himself was unaware" (Freud, 1909d, p. 167). In this case, the satisfaction is paradoxically felt as displeasure. This is also the case for symptoms, nightmares, and certain bungled actions. With the witticism on the other hand, one can immediately see how the effect of signification brings satisfaction instead.

This means that the formations of the unconscious are caught in a double movement that is both semantic and economic, that is to say, they stem from both the symptom and the drive (Miller, 2001b). They go from a "minus" of meaning to a "plus" of meaning, and from displeasure to the production of a satisfaction (*cf.* "The sense of symptoms" and "The paths to the formation of symptoms" in Freud 1916–1917). This paradoxical satisfaction felt as displeasure corresponds to the Lacanian concept of jouissance. Freud forged the myth of the drives to account for this. The real aspect of this "myth" is the Real of libido. The term "myth" does not for all that disqualify the concept. It simply indicates the necessity of a more rigorous formulation. The Real of jouissance is particularised by the fact of eluding symbolisation. Only a small portion can be rendered in logic, and this is why Freud and, later, Lacan were continually reformulating this concept throughout their respective teachings.

The concept of the drive is defined in Freud's 1915 metapsychological papers as "a concept on the borderline between the mental and the physical" (Freud, 2005a, p. 16). From the biology of his time Freud borrows the differentiation of two types of cell—sexual and non-sexual—to account for two kinds of drive that he initially calls "sexual drives" and "ego-preservation drives" (ibid., pp. 18–20). In the second part of his work, at the turning point of the 1920s, he will call them "life drives" and "death drives" (Section IV of Freud, 1920g). The crux of the matter is not the dated biological reference, but libido. The economy of this libido would later be reformulated by Lacan.

Man and animal

Widlöcher sets out to efface the differences between the drive and instinct. The concept of drive is, however, distinct from that of instinct, first and foremost by dint of the fact that the drive specifies what is human whilst instinct is proper to the animal realm. Animal organisms are endowed with an innate knowledge. In man, the drives are not only a form of knowledge, they are also a form of truth. Yet, this knowledge is unfamiliar to the subject because it is enciphered in metaphors and metonymies. As for truth, it is repressed because its consequences are unbearable for the subject. Therefore it returns in the symptom. One can say that psychical symptoms manifest the return of a repressed truth that is bound to libido with its dual values of desire and jouissance.[1] We might add that the truth of desire is bound to the Real of drive jouissance.

Of all living creatures, the human being is the only one to suffer truth. How are we to account for this? Precisely by distinguishing between knowledge and truth, and then by articulating truth and jouissance. In speaking beings, the organism's instinctual knowledge interferes with the truth, which is why there is no instinct to guide them. What they are left with is the drive, the myth that reflects the interference of both truth and knowledge back onto the living being: the truth-effects of speech are imprisoned in the symptom, and they serve the constant production of drive jouissance. Instinct allows animals to preserve their life adequately and to ensure the survival of the species. In wild animals, instinctual need is not open to eroticisation. A lion, for example, will not kill for pleasure, but only to eat, and he knows nothing of anorexia, insomnia, and impotence. As for the lioness that mates with him, she knows nothing of jealousy. Things would certainly be a lot different if she knew how to count to three.

Body and organism

Back in his *Studies on Hysteria*, Freud related the cases of some of his female patients and their bodily sufferings. Several suffered from paralysed legs, even though, as Freud realised, the organism as such was not concerned in these symptoms. They had indeed stopped walking, and they did indeed suffer, but their symptoms were linked to the word "leg" and bore no relation to the muscles, nerves, arteries, and veins that go to make up a leg and which turned out to unaffected by any lesion. Moreover, hysterical paralyses do not follow any neurological trajectory. This is why Freud was able to say that the hysteric's body is a body affected by language and ignorant of anatomy. The hysteric suffers from the word, and not the organ. The most cursory experience of psychoanalysis confirms these facts.

A case of hysterical blindness published by Freud and commented on by Jacques-Alain Miller shows this logic at work (Miller, 2001b). Normally the eye would serve to preserve the organism (ego-preservation drives) by warning it of a visible danger, but in this case the eyes are put in the service of the pleasure of seeing a forbidden scene (partial sexual drive). When the organ stops functioning for the preservation of the organism, it forces its way through (with respect to its normal functioning) to satisfy the auto-erotic imperative of drive jouissance. The blindness is sanctioning the body for the excessive pleasure it has felt. What Freud here calls sexual pleasure is the pleasure of the organ as it steals away from its living finality, to the point of completely abolishing it in paralysis. Pleasure has transformed into jouissance, vouching for a satisfaction and a suffering that are steadfastly bound to one another. In this way, ethics necessarily enters the realm of Freudian and Lacanian *biology*.

Across the whole of his oeuvre Freud upholds the idea that there are two types of drive. Lacan went on to unite them while nonetheless upholding the distinction between organism and body. In so far as it is made from language and is erotised, the body doubles up on the organism. To agree with Freud when he says that the concept of the drive is "a concept on the borderline between the mental and the physical" is to accept that the organism cannot explain away the psychical symptom. If one is to account for it, one has to make room for the libidinalised speaking body. This has consequences, in particular the fact that the drive finds constant satisfaction in both the symptom and the suffering it inflicts.

To account for libidinal economy, Freud builds the concept of the drive from four *constant* elements that define it: its thrust, its source, its aim and its object (Freud, 2005a, pp. 17–18). The thrust is a *constant* force that exists in every living being who speaks. Therefore the drive is different from need (indicated by instinct) which diminishes when satisfied (like hunger after the ingestion of food). The drive's source is in the body: for there to be jouissance, there has to be a living body. As for the drive's object, it is indifferent because what matters to it is the goal of satisfaction, which is invariably reached whether in pleasure or displeasure. One can grasp why Lacan said that the subject is always happy (Lacan, 1990a, p. 22): however the symptom expresses itself, whatever suffering the subject must bear, the drive always finds satisfaction in it.

The lock

Science does not and cannot make any room for jouissance. This is why the would-be "scientific" conversion of psychoanalysis necessitates a revision of the concept of the drive. Widlöcher thus had the idea of doing away with the concept by replacing the noun *pulsion* ("drive") with the adjective *pulsionnel*. This switch is barely perceptible at the lexical level, but the conceptual consequence is far-reaching. How is this to be explained? The neurosciences rule out any biological foundation to the drive, and quite rightly so. Widlöcher follows them, but he also rejects the libido's economy. In other words, for him the drive is neither a biology, nor an energetics, nor an economy. It would merely be a myth from which no real could emerge. Widlöcher thus asserts that the drive is the epistemological lock that has to be forced open so that psychoanalysis may finally become a cognitive "science" (Wildlöcher, 1996, p. 69). Indeed, Widlöcher wants a *"pulsionnel* without *pulsion"* (Widlöcher, 2003, p. 171) in order to force a way through to science. This *pulsionnel* qualifies the "thought-act" because, "any act, including thought, has the property of tending towards its realisation" (Widlöcher, 1986, p. 57). And so, he adds, one can do away with the drive.

For good measure, the four elements that define the drive—thrust, source, goal, and object—are redefined as properties of the "thought-act". Thrust and source are thus *intentionality* while the object is tied to the goal. From this perspective, there is nothing left of the Real of libido that Freud formalised to account for the jouissance that singularises the human being.

After carving up thought in order to write off libido, Widlöcher next tries to convince us that we have exaggerated the importance that child sexuality and narcissism had for Freud (Wildöcher, 2000, pp. 1–55). This leads him to confuse human jouissance and animal satisfaction. In 1986, his rejection of the drive favoured the recycling of the conditioned reflexes that were being endorsed by adherents of CBT. Ten years later, the same rejection of libido is being made to serve as a stepping-stone to Bowlby's ethology (preface to Guedeney & Guedeney, 2006, p. vii). After lab rats and test dogs, it is the turn of the monkeys to rush to the aid of the psychological scientist and rescue the idea of homogeneity of satisfaction, be it human or animal. Let's give some credit to the animals, however, who know nothing of the savagery of rape and other morbid delectations—and if only it stopped there.

The CBT key

So, the *pulsionnel* has to be made to serve the takeover of the Freudian heritage. It must work towards the consecration of the conditioned reflex perfected by Ivan Pavlov and taken up by B. F. Skinner. However, in straying off into these Daedalian flights of fancy, our Icarus has climbed so high up the measuring scales that he is spelling his own downfall into the muddy maze of animal experimentation (Widlöcher, 1995, p. 217, *passim*). Here, there is no longer any difference between Pavlov's dog and Skinner's conditioned man. For Pavlov and Skinner, conditioned reflexes are enough to account for the complexity of the jouissance of human beings. From this perspective, the many wars down through history will have to find another cause besides the death drive, which these thinkers deem meaningless. As for the ego-preserving drives, once they have been reduced to simple instinctive needs they no longer amount to anything. Without the eroticisation of needs such as hunger, how is one to grasp the logic of anorexia or bulimia? The vomiting of young anorexics does not have a univocal value, and they won't stop under enforced authority. For some of them, when the truth of the love that they are force-fed comes to be uttered, the necessity of making themselves its martyr can dissipate. Though the voice of reason is hushed, it persists so long as it has not been heard. When it comes to the sexual drives, they are no better off in Widlöcher's theory because they have to restrict themselves to reproductive need. Doesn't this fall rather short when it comes to giving an account of the diversity of modes of jouissance, both hetero- and homosexual? And how is the reproductive purpose to be entertained in shoe fetishists?

Truth silenced

Elucidating the logic of jouissance is not of course at issue in this kind of project. This is why, contrary to the facts of the analytic experience, Widlöcher asserts: "Psychoanalysis does not have the goal of establishing or acknowledging a truth" (Widlöcher, 1996, p. 194). The silenced truth, which proved to be the key to the psychical symptom, is thus swept aside, leaving no further objection to humans being conditioned like lab rats, in keeping with CBT ideology. Once these fanciful notions have borne their fruit, there is no longer any opposition between words and libido. Freud's metapsychology is definitively ruled out in favour of Widlöcher's "metapsychology of meaning".

When he formulated Freud and Lacan's position on this subject, Jacques-Alain Miller said the drive must be acknowledged "as a kind of activity that imposes itself on representations and controls them to its own ends" (Miller, 2001b). This is what Widlöcher refuses, judging it inconceivable that "a demand from the body should impose on the mind the initiative and sense of action" (Widlöcher, 1986, p. 47).

With Freud and Lacan

This way of proceeding calls for at least three remarks. First, Widlöcher's *pulsionnel* blurs the boundary between Being and body, and thereby fails to recognise the satisfaction linked to words, that is to say, the link between signifiers and enjoy-meant.[2] No sooner has he denied this jouissance than it starts cropping up constantly in Widlöchian thought to the point that it could be qualified as a *pensée pulsionnelle*. We repeat: with scant regard for the complexity of the fundamental concepts of psychoanalysis, each concept is transformed into "thought": the unconscious is thought, desire is a thought, the drive, and so on and so forth. How can one fail to spot the autoerotic imperative of the drive in this overinvestment of thought? Isn't Widlöcher actively demonstrating the force of the very drive he means to combat, to wit, an eroticisation of the thoughts that elude animal instinct?

Second, denying the opposition between words and libido amounts to denying the action of words on the body. The action of the signifier is twofold: on the one hand it mortifies the living being, and on the other, it makes the jouissance seep out of him. Lacan sets out this logic with his concept of discourse in *Seminar XVII* (Lacan, 2007), though in his previous seminar he was already indicating that what goes amiss in sexuality cannot be *expressed* by the unconscious, but merely *indicated* by the unconscious through the objects of the drive. One should say that the unconscious "does not speak" sexuality, in the same way that we say someone doesn't speak English or French, but with the proviso that the unconscious "speaks about" sexuality with the objects *a* of the drive that it produces and which stand in a relation of metonymy and metaphor to sexuality. Thus it would be wrong to claim that there is no theory of the drives in Lacan's teaching (Widlöcher, 2003, p. 242). On the contrary, this concept was being constantly reformulated, right up to its ultimate simplification in *Seminar XXIII* where it is defined as "the echo in the body of a fact of saying" (Lacan, 2016).

Third and finally, we shall say it again: Widlöcher's *pulsionnel* brings about a foreclosure of truth. Life bound to instinctual knowledge alone effectively excludes any entanglements with truth and its bond with the erotised body. Rejecting truth and the Real brings about a foreclosure of the concept of the drive. The objective certitude that is so eagerly being sought can no longer concern the libidinal body, but only the organism. The Real of jouissance is replaced by the reality of the organs to which medicine attends. On the other hand, for the analytic experience in the Lacanian orientation, truth, with its dialectical and variable nature, can at the end of the analytic experience reach a certitude that has the value of a Real. It is then accessible to a singular but rigorous demonstration. With this in mind, Lacan proposed in 1967 that the psychoanalysts of his school might give an account of what they had learnt from their analysis to a scientific committee, by means of a procedure he called "the Pass" (Lacan, 1995).

Anxiety

Anxiety has held a special place among the affects from the start because it signals the original trauma.

The original trauma

Freud made his theory of repression revolve around anxiety. In the first part of his work, he isolated the fact that repression causes anxiety (Freud, 1915d, 1915e). Then, with the turning point of the 1920s, he was trying to understand why symptoms are increasingly resistant to interpretation, leading analyses to become longer and longer. He then isolated another kind of anxiety, a primitive kind, which is not the *effect* but the *cause* of repression (Freud, 1926d). He named this anxiety "castration anxiety". In fact, this is the keystone to his discovery. Let's leave to one side the detail of his developments, and simply note one of the decisive consequences of this modification of the theory of anxiety (required by the practice of the analytic experience). In the first formalisation of anxiety, repression could be imputed to the Other in general (upbringing, society, etc.). With the second formalisation of anxiety, this is out of the question. One cannot entertain the idea that upbringing might modify a subject's relation to what constitutes his anxiety. In the Freudian corpus, castration anxiety has different forms: seduction, the threat of castration, the Oedipus complex, the observation of parental coitus, the loss of love, all of which are traumas that produce traces of affect in general and of anxiety in particular.

For Lacan, the necessary trauma that leaves these traces of affect in its wake is the trauma that language inflicts on the body of the speaking being. This trauma does not arise through the fault of the parents, nor any other party. The signifier alone induces castration and produces jouissance. Language is both that which mortifies the living being, inflicting upon him a "minus" of jouissance, a castration of jouissance, and that which produces a jouissance to be recuperated. Lacan calls the object of this recuperation: the object *a*, "surplus jouissance". The Lacanian object *a* carries with it these two values: on one hand, an emptiness, a lack, which the drive turns around, and on the other, the production of jouissance obtained from the body's rim zones. These rims are articulated with objects such as the voice, the gaze, and so on.

One of the functions of anxiety is to signal the emergence of the object *a* in a register to which it does not naturally belong. Anxiety signals the necessity of a separation from a jouissance that is making the subject suffer. Therefore, it is a sign of the Real, and this is why Lacan distinguishes it from all the other affects as being the only one that does not deceive (Lacan, 2014b).

Cognitivising Darwin

The rejection of anxiety is thus another step on the way to imposing the idea that neither the body nor jouissance have any existence, and that nothing exists but the organism and animal satisfaction ("Le langage de l'angoisse" in Widlöcher, 1986, pp. 101–128).[3] Darwin and Hume, both of whom are revisited for the occasion, are drafted in to guarantee the enterprise. From Darwinism, Widlöcher gets the idea that affects are supposedly residues of once useful behaviour. As for Hume, he pushed the consequences of empiricism so far that he dissolved the Real of the cause. Thus, the only relation of causality that facts allow him to assert resides in thought association. We know that for Hume the flame might not be the cause of the burn. The burn and the flame are merely two associated thoughts.

You will have grasped the nature of the interest that Hume can hold for Widlöcher. Hume asserts that we do not *feel* happiness when we see a friend, but that we *think* on this idea with happiness (Widlöcher, 1986, p. 102). Thus, for him, affects are not to be differentiated. Anxiety ceases to be a quality and becomes an assessable quantity, this being the fate he sets in store for all affects. It is no longer a question of recognising them as deceptive, as Lacan does; whatever the affect may be (fear, fright, happiness, woe, etc.) it qualifies a thought. For the most part, they are supposed to be passed down by heredity, the rest being acquired through learning (learning that is more or less faulty according to received wisdom). Poor upbringing would thus have the power to modify both the human brain and the "instincts". In this weird science, psychology and biology stand in continuity. Anxiety no longer signals the man with his worries and concerns, it becomes a stage in the hereditary programming of thoughts. There would be nothing more to say about it beyond what can be seen (i.e., rapid breathing that needs to be slowed down).

In the form it is taken up here, Darwinism invariably serves a narrow hereditary conception of human behaviour. With its new makeover, it contributes to the dissolution of castration anxiety, which is no longer considered to be the cause of repression. Moreover, repression itself ceases to be the *judgement of the subject who decides to flee what bothers him*, which produces a psychical symptom. Once the real cause of repression has been dissolved, Widlöcher's Humean empiricism leads him to explain affects by thought association alone.

Aping Hume

Once again, Bowlby's monkeys are supposed to convince us of the kinship between man and animal. The lessons from animal ethology applied to humans hold the dubious interest of aping Hume while biologising him. The questions that each of us may pose concerning ourselves and our destinies, and the answers we may come up with, are reduced to mere "stimulus-response" reflex arcs. Judgements and beliefs thus become superfluous for the new decerebrated race that we are being asked to join without further ado.

The difference between an objective danger (such as the fear of falling) and a subjective danger (such as the fear of losing the love of a loved one) no longer exists. Thus unified, danger is inserted into a genetic programme. Once a danger has been perceived, it triggers a "stimulus-response" reflex: the danger "stimulus" first triggers the adapted response of "thought-affect" and then the "thought-behaviour" response. Fear, anxiety, fright, depression, and all other affects, are likewise transformed into *thought*. In this simplex system born of CBT cogitation, but which is utterly foreign to science, it is not certain whether the naked eye distinguishes as yet between thoughts and hormones.

The symptom as a bargaining tool

Sadness is not always a symptom. Freud explained this, in particular in his text "Mourning and melancholia" (Freud, 2005b) which constitutes part of his metapsychology. This article turns out to be the bastion to which Widlöcher has laid unrelenting siege in the hope of imposing the biopsychosocial idea of the symptom as backed by pro-CBT psychiatry (Widlöcher, 1995, p. 247;[4] Widlöcher & Hardy, 1991; Widlöcher, 1994, p. 3). We shall be coming back to this in a later chapter so for now we shall limit ourselves to just a few observations on this topic.

What today goes by the name of "depression" is a vast ragbag that fails to distinguish between the sadness of mourning and the sadness of melancholia. Freud draws a strong contrast between them, however, based on the economy of libido, and shows how the bond that links truth and libido is functioning in neurotic sadness but broken in psychotic melancholia. In Widlöcher's theory, these symptoms are muddled up in a single symptom named "depression". This metamorphosed *symptom* would just be yet another faulty thought in need of correction.

Widlöcher has even drawn up his own assessment questionnaires to measure "depression *per se*" on a scale. At one end of the scale we find "light anxiety" (which has been plucked from the neuroses) and at the other, religious melancholic delusions (taken from the psychoses). Therefore, a patient who believes in an auditory hallucination telling him that he is the reincarnation of the Son and the Holy Ghost is no longer recognised as delusional, but as endowed with "depressive spirituality" (Widlöcher, 1995, p. 9). This entire lucubration is to be proved by the efficacy of CBT, with anti-depressants being prescribed to all and sundry.

As for the other symptoms fabricated by biopsychosocial psychiatry, they also derive from this model. Phobias are due to poor educative conditioning; the psychoses have no more pertinence; and the neuroses are obsolete, becoming personality disorders with hereditary predisposition.

Freud invented obsessional neurosis. It didn't exist before him. If one is only to retain one element of the obsessional-neurotic symptom, the one that says most for many humans, it would surely be the subject's relation to a desire that has been rendered impossible. This manifests itself in the subject's love life by the doubling of the love object: the idealised woman of desire, "the lady of my thoughts" whom the subject thinks about all the time without ever being able to enjoy her; and the woman who is not loved but whom he can enjoy at the price of a certain debasement. The symptoms of obsessional neurosis, such as nagging ideas and compulsive actions, stem from the impossibility that the subject feels when it comes to conjoining love, desire, and jouissance in one same partner. For each subject, obsessional symptoms are caused by an economy of libido that differs depending on whether a neurosis or a psychosis is involved. In the eyes of the former president of Freud's Association, however, obsession is one single entity: OCD (Obsessive compulsive disorder). And its cause would be a genetic serotonin deficiency.[5]

Neurological symptoms do not fall within the province of psychoanalysis, nor does the study of hormonal secretions or their genetic programming. If psychical symptoms can be undone by speech it is because their cause depends on language. This is not the case for genetics, which for now at least is impermeable to the effects of language. The cause of the symptom stems from an unconscious choice on the part of the subject, an "unsoundable decision of Being" (Lacan,

2006, p. 145), and it makes no place for the theory of the hereditary degeneration of the symptom. Freud was unswervingly emphatic in his criticism of the hypocrisy of those who subscribed to such theories. Note, too, that a symptom is always incomparable. Each symptom stands as the sign of a subject's absolute singularity, his way of striking a compromise with the jouissance that inhabits him. Furthermore, it would be wrong to consider that the symptom can be objectified: the analyst does not stand outside the symptom, he must complete it from within in order to make it analysable and bring the patient's unconscious into existence.

Lastly, the evaluated subject loses his singularity. Statistical evaluation of symptoms is quite foreign to the Freudian discipline, but it does conform to the ideology of the CBT therapeutic contract. In the wishful words of Daniel Widlöcher, evaluation is out to bring the Freudian discipline in line with "the common market of cognitive sciences" (Widlöcher, 1996, p. 95).

Executing psychoanalysis

Thus executed, psychoanalysis becomes, for Widlöcher, a treatment of the symptom that consists first in convincing patients that their thinking is askew and then in educating them to think straight (i.e., to think as their shrink thinks). This is what the analytic experience is supposed to become: a mental orthopaedics claiming to make people think differently by establishing new neuronal connections (Widlöcher, 1996, p. 244) or, to use Widlöcher's terms, to "widen the analysand's mental universe". In this reformulation of the evolution of the species, some day we will doubtless manage to shed light on the shift from *Mémoires d'un âne* to Spinoza's *Ethics*.

Ultimately treating rather lightly his fear of a dilution of psychoanalysis into the various existing psychotherapies, the former president of the IPA now considers these therapies to be the most useful ones. According to him, "scientific" psychoanalysis, just like CBT and other therapeutic relaxations, favours the actions of the genetic programme which now accounts for the unconscious. The different classes of medication (anxiolytics, anti-depressants, neuroleptics) are also supposed to have an influence on this programme. The efficacy of these treatments has to stand in for the (still wanting) evidence for the scientific foundation of these outlandish theories.

One particular remark by the former IPA president will be enough to grasp the rhetoric of this concession that aims to pass off the scientistic viewpoint for what it would like to be: "objective certitude". The more he foregrounds its gaps, the more value he believes he can ascribe to its strange assertions:

> We are still very poorly acquainted with the ontogenesis of the sequential programmes: to what extent can one speak of an innate programme and the role of the experience of environment? We are likewise very poorly acquainted with the regulating mechanisms. How is the execution of the programme put in place? (Widlöcher, 1986, pp. 126–127)

Might these nagging thoughts be the signature of an untreatable Nemesis?

Good practice

For Freud and Lacan, the practice and the theory of psychoanalysis are inseparable. Mindful as he was of consequences, each obstacle that Freud met in his practice led him to reformulate his theory. Similarly, Lacan's teaching is none other than a theory of analytic practice. Today, Jacques-Alain Miller's *Lacanian Orientation* is breathing life into the analytic discourse and ensuring the solidity of the World Association of Psychoanalysis.

Babel

As we have seen, Freud founded the IPA in order to keep the discipline of psychoanalysis on track. Those psychoanalysts who judged it productive joined the Association. To begin with, everyone spoke the same language. They grew and multiplied. Fairly quickly, emboldened by their qualifications, a few of them wanted to lead the psychoanalytic people to reach loftier heights. This goal of elevation did not sit well with their conceptual bric-a-brac. Under the sway of the university clan won over to CBT, they found out how to cross the threshold of the visible, but not the threshold of the ethical mind. These heights remained shut off from them. From that point forth, confusion reigned. It turned into a kind of Babel. The IPA was torn into divergent theoretical currents that formed different languages familiar to some and incomprehensible for others, compromising its homogeneous and peaceful existence.

The new heteroclite enterprise could no longer keep the secret of the impossibility of defining the psychoanalyst. (It has to be said that Lacan had dared to divulge it, and his teaching had already spread the news to the four corners of the earth.) Being fitted out by the same tailor and wearing the same suit each day was no longer enough to ensure that the members of the IPA were cut from the same cloth. Besides, had that been the case, how would they have imposed this fashion on all those who were put off by the uniform? To clear away the obstacle and restore peace, they came up with the idea of forming a clan that would ensure the hegemony of the empire by affirming one self-same practice in order to make the IPA the sole orthodox psychoanalytic populace.

Questions of identity

In France, they had to wait for Lacan's death at the beginning of the 1980s before this policy could be implemented. Widlöcher then tried to impose on the IPA the unilateral thinking of a "straight up" practice: his own. The enemy (and there can be little doubt that these were the Lacanian analysts) would have to be fought mercilessly. Lacanian theory counted for little more than the other theoretical currents represented in the IPA, but being free of any standard, and unjustly accused of being free of principle, it would have to be denounced for having threatened to remind them that there is no possible definition of the *Being* of the psychoanalyst (who exists through his act alone). Now, this scientistic montage was formed precisely so that the problem of the analytic act (introduced by Freud and then conceptualised by Lacan) would never be posed.

Widlöcher asserts, however, that defining the psychoanalyst is a problem-free task inasmuch as he identifies the analyst with his own idea of one. His book *Métapsychologie du sens* (Widlöcher, 1986), was set to become the dogma that will found this new orthodoxy capable of safeguarding a "scientific" practice of analysis. He writes that we need "to exorcise this phantom model" (Freud's metapsychology) that has "polluted our 'psychological' intuitions" (Widlöcher, 1986, p. 55). This pollution would be Freud's doing. Meanwhile, "straight up" thinking is to be ascribed to Widlöcher. It is under the cover of this fortification that over these last thirty years the destiny of the forced cognitivisation of psychoanalysis has been forged in the IPA.

The fundamental rule

As outlined above, the necessary and sufficient condition for the existence of the analytic experience is respect for the fundamental rule, which stipulates that during the session the analysand should commit to saying everything that occurs to him, without leaving anything out, even if it seems embarrassing, incongruous, or unrelated to what he was saying beforehand. This is the only rule Freud formulated for analytic practice, and he devised it because the symptom only thrives when it is concealed and fed by the patient's critical judgement, which therefore has to be suspended during the session. Free association is an invitation to the analysand to *say things well*. It is also the door through which he enters the psychoanalytic ethic.

Widlöcher's gift for churning out postulates promptly transformed the fundamental rule into *thought* transfer. For him, the rule could not concern the analysand alone, because then "it would produce nothing of interest" (Widlöcher, 2003, p. 46). It must also be applied to the psychoanalyst. The patient observes his thoughts, then he relates them to the analyst who has to listen to them, but not necessarily respond. Now, what distinguishes a psychoanalyst from a simple confident is precisely the fact that he becomes his patient's partner through his responses to the manifestation of a symptom, interpreting it so as to scale it down and make it vanish. This is why Lacan developed the concept of the analytic act. It has to be said that Widlöcher's ideas leave no place for this concept. Instead he allows himself to confess that the ideal session would be one of dyadic silence (Widlöcher, 1996, p. 147). Is it not the desire to impose silence on the Freudian discipline itself that is being hinted at here?

In the theory of Widlöchian mental functioning, thinking entails a reciprocal associative labour over an infinite session time. Indeed, there will never be a sufficient amount of thoughts to censure desire and to reject the logic of jouissance. Once the bond between analysand and analyst has become *a dyadic relationship*, the unconscious is excluded by a mutual knowledge or a "common cognitive environment" (Widlöcher, 1996, p. 104).

Telepathy

Widlöcher's thinking machine knows no bounds. Countertransference, transference, and interpretation are each in turn transformed into *thoughts*. Though absent from the Freudian corpus, countertransference[6] complements the revised form of free association. What floats to the surface in "free-floating attention" actively contributes to the "co-thinking" that transference has become (Widlöcher, 1996, p. 151; Widlöcher, 2003, p. 21; Widlöcher & Miller, 2002, p. 23; Widlöcher, 1962, p. 12). According to the former IPA president, Freud shrank back from acknowledging the true nature of transference. He did not dare to formulate transference in terms of thought transfer, that is to say, telepathy. Widlöchean co-thinking remedies this shortcoming (Widlöcher, 1996, pp. 158–159). As for interpretation, now defined as a partial fusing of two trains of thought, it would be a shared thought, an echo of the patient's thinking (ibid., p. 149). This would require an extended session length in order to think, imagine, and feel ... How could that be doubted?

A real belief in telepathy or co-thinking[7] is seldom met outside the field of the psychoses. Distinguishing either of them from a scientistic delusion would be fairly arduous, but this does offer a better grasp of this recourse to occultism. Rather than opting for an engagement in psychoanalysis, occultism has to exclude desire and the productions of desire from reality. Thus, instead of following the path opened by Freud, this scientism, by lying in wait for the moment when it might free itself from the constraints of acknowledged scientific laws, conveys the hope that other laws of nature might emerge so that it may bow down to them. In the meantime, it makes do with a few imprecise propositions.

Standardised practice thus becomes the experimental condition for measuring the different forms of knowledge in *psychological science*, allowing them to be assessed and compared. Doubt and wariness can then feed on endless checking procedures since, for Widlöcher the positivist, it sounds very much like one can trust neither in the patient's judgment nor in that of the IPA-trained psychoanalyst who will never be sufficiently objective (Widlöcher, 1996, p. 23). Of course, the advantage of a standardised practice is that it imposes a fixed-length session and then "scientifically" rejects the Lacanian practice. The stopwatch of science must be applicable to all, without exception. Is it necessary to call to mind that medical science has demonstrated that no biological rhythm whatsoever conforms to this timekeeping?

These are, however, rules of "good practice", which have been set up as moral instructions. For our positivist psychoanalyst Widlöcher, the analysand's speech runs the risk of introducing deviations into practice, deviations that need to be avoided at any cost. Furthermore, intentional thought turns the unconscious into a "meaning to do" and promotes an ethics of intention. In stark contrast to this approach, for Freud but also for Lacan and the psychoanalysts of his School, the analysand's speech lies at the heart of the analytic experience.

Punctuations

Four points will suffice to clarify the reasons for the latter position.

1. First of all, in the Lacanian orientation, standardised practice is insufficient when it comes to circumscribing the Being of the psychoanalyst because Being is impossible to define. What exists, as we have seen, is the analytic act. It does not depend on universal rules, but on the singular focus of the analyst's desire in his own analysis. This is why the fundamental rule only concerns the analysand. On the side of the analyst there is no fundamental rule. He is not to say whatever comes into his mind because what he says bears a consequence. He must, therefore, take into account the effects of his speech. Interpretation comes under the heading of the analytic act, and like any act, it is desubjectivised. It does not fall on the side of thought, but on the side of the rejection of thought. It does not require an infinite time of reflection that lies out on a horizon from which all doubt will have vanished. To be a good hearer is enough when it comes to interpreting because certainty is generated by the act itself and its consequences, not by the infinite accumulation of knowledge.
2. The psychoanalyst's mental experience is thus excluded from the session. Lacanian practice does not dabble with countertransference and is thereby coherent with the variable-length session and the doctrine of the unconscious conceived of as a "meaning to say" and a "meaning to enjoy", and not as a "meaning to do".
3. This means that the ethics of psychoanalysis is an ethics of consequences, and not one of intentions. The consequences of his acts are what allow the subject to know what he wants.

4. Lastly, the eroticised temporality of the unconscious is singular to each subject. The obsessional's procrastination has little in common with the hysteric's get-up-and-go or the slowdown of the melancholic. Moreover, this singularity, which binds Being and time together, varies in accordance with a logical temporality that stems from a topology that knows nothing of clockwork time. Therefore, we should also add that the "scientific" psychoanalysis Widlöcher is calling for brings about a foreclosure of time as well.

What's one more contradiction to Daniel Widlöcher? He claims to be forcing psychoanalysis into the domain of science, but to do so he goes looking for support in Hume, who rejected any dogmatic idea of science. What seems to matter to Widlöcher above all else is to transform as many psychoanalytic concepts as possible (the unconscious, desire, anxiety) into *thought* and to reject all the rest (such as the *subject*, which is a negative magnitude, or jouissance, which escapes words).

An ethical wager

The river of sludge

The "scientific" revision of psychoanalysis brings with it a conception of man as transparent to himself. All philosophy is built on the model of the ideology of perception, whose principle is the illusion of the subject of cognisance. In his fourteenth seminar (Lacan, 1966–1967), Lacan compared it to a male "fabrication" that pertains to a certain impotence because it denies the *minus* proper to the cause of desire, mistaking it for a zero. Scientistic mysticism thus bears the stamp of the rejection of castration in its assertion that everything may be known about any human being, right down to his inmost Being.

The symptom cannot be reduced to mere satisfaction. It is always a repetition of sexual satisfaction, and this is the crux of the Freudian discovery. Freud held firmly to this certainty because he did not want to see a shallow theory of the psyche slipping back into the rut of occultism (which he put down to a spellbound Jung). Contrary to scientistic mysticism, the *analytic discourse* takes on board the impossibility of writing the sexual relationship (which makes for the dignity of the psychical symptom inherent to each and every human) and labours to draw the right lessons from it.

The sacrificing of the Freudian discipline is aimed at the dissolution of the Real of jouissance, a real that pierces a hole in knowledge and causes a divided subject. The flaw in knowledge cannot, however, be reduced. Sealing it over with more science is the dead-end solution offered by the university discourse that tries to master the subject's jouissance. To bring out the Real at stake, the only solution is to accord a functional role to speech within the *analytic discourse*. Indeed, this is the only discourse that allows for the articulation of the subject and his cause. The cognitivisation of psychoanalysis, though undertaken with an eye to saving it, constitutes a serious error in orientation. Blinkered tactics and costly strategies have been serving a policy that is born of a psychology that has strayed off into the deleterious mirages of transparency in the service of the modern master.

The foreclosure of the names of Lacan and Freud

Lacan did not simply preserve the Freudian discipline. Through his orientation he was able to give it a fresh momentum that still propels it today. He was made to pay for this faultless determination in 1964, at the price of his excommunication from the IPA. Widlöcher was one of Lacan's analysands, and played a role in his excommunication. In other words, his rejection of Lacan's teaching is not something new.[8] He has been labouring away at the foreclosure of Lacan's name, and his teaching along with it, for nigh on half a century.

Widlöcher has undertaken a methodical revision of the Freudian corpus, effectively pulverising it. Psychoanalysis teaches us that the subject comes to know what he truly desires through the consequences of his acts. If we want to be coherent with the Freudian discovery, we must therefore admit that Widlöcher's publications should be judged on the fruit they bear, and not their premises. When he became president of the IPA, he took on a commitment to serve the Freudian discipline. By what strange irony of history did he become an architect of the foreclosure of Freud's name and teaching, spelling doom for psychoanalysis?

A reformulation of the Freudian concepts is doubtless called for, but not one that sweeps aside the jouissance of which the human being is made. Bleuler wanted as much in his time. You will recall that instead of the Freudian concept of auto-eroticism, he favoured the term "autism" because the contraction of the words sounded less shocking to prudish ears. We remember too Freud's verdict: "If you give way on the words, you give way on the things." Isn't the same thing being confirmed with

Widlöcher's revision? He has given way on the words to such an extent that Freud's name is starting to bother him. Nothing more remains of psychoanalysis but the threatened signifier, which Widlöcher is now trying to replace with that of *psychodynamic psychotherapy*.[9] The intention to debate (Widlöcher, 2008) is in itself praiseworthy, but what kind of debate is possible with those who want the psychoanalytic discourse to vanish from the face of the earth?

The politics of the unconscious

The psychical symptom is always a response to the dominant discourse. The dominant discourse is felt as a kind of unease because it cannot make any room for the singularity of each subject. It is legitimate, therefore, to say that there is no clinic of the subject without a clinic of civilisation. The symptom is wholly taken up in civilisation, but this does not make it wholly social: it belongs to the subject. Today, the biopsychosocial conception of symptoms is rejecting what is most particular in the psychical symptom and is shifting the demand from the sufferer towards the social sphere. Lacan's thesis that *what is foreclosed from the symbolic comes back in the real* enables us to predict how the clinic will assume new social forms, forms that will remain enigmatic for the master. Therefore they will have to be interpreted. Isn't this already the case with the unexplained violence that some subjects are demonstrating? The psychoses that often afflict them, and which too often go unrecognised, are reduced to the rank of "psychopathy" by the advocates of pro-CBT psychiatry. New symptoms are emerging in the shape of hysterical epidemics, such as extraterrestrial sightings in the US or the anorexia-bulimia epidemics spreading across the democratic countries, that is to say, anywhere where homes have household refrigerators to give consistency to a universe in which there can be no more lack. The politics of the unconscious is a politics of symptoms, and it indicates a series of issues.

The first issue is the training of psychoanalysts. This is something Lacan always took very seriously. It is all the more critical today given that his school has been officially recognised as an institution of public benefit. The procedure of the Pass stands in some sense as an auto-assessment that a psychoanalyst can put before his peers for validation so as to become an analyst of Lacan's school. An analysand who has seen his analysis through to the end can take it upon himself to raise the singularity of his case to the rigour of the matheme. Such a step testifies to the requirement of scientific rigour in order to reach the Real of structure. Lacan's school also proposes another assessment that guarantees the psychoanalyst's training. It is not requested by the psychoanalyst himself. His peers are the ones who decide to confer the title based on the results of his practice and his publications. As for applied psychoanalysis, it seems to have found an assessment regime that embraces short therapies of Lacanian orientation too. This is particularly the case in the Psychoanalytic Centres for Consultation and Treatment which are open to all and free of charge. They exist up and down France and also much further afield.[10]

The next issue is the politics of psychoanalysis. It concerns the schools of the WAP (World Association of Psychoanalysis) and its links with other professional associations like the IPA. Ongoing commentary on the analytic movement and its publications remains crucial, lest we should once again run the risk of being taken by surprise, as was the case with the ruling on the psychotherapies. The IPA is home to currents that do not necessarily subscribe to the pro-CBT university bent. This is especially true for the North American current of intersubjectivity which is seeing a revival in interest for the subject (*cf.* Laurent, 2014, pp. 127–140).

The issue is also and above all the transmission of the analytic discourse to future generations. Today, we can say that the IPA's pro-CBT university current has pushed the consequences of empiricism so far that, on the one hand, it is no longer able to uphold its critical function in this regard, and on the other, it has awoken us from our dogmatic slumber. This route through psychoanalytic doctrine affords an insight into Lacan's school and the way in which it alone upholds this function, which is so crucial for the survival of psychoanalysis. Indeed, in this day and age, it is Lacan's school that stands as the orthodoxy. Moreover, the danger that now threatens it is one of dogmatism. This danger lies in wait for us, unless we agree to sidestep routine and favour invention. Such a step is unthinkable without a teaching that is careful to avoid fetishising the concepts, so as to go on ceaselessly reinventing itself.

There can be no doubt that Widlöcher is merely a symptom of the present time. The attacks on psychoanalysis that we have seen in France go beyond his person. Nevertheless, if his publications hold some importance, it is in so far as they represent a certain psychoanalytic *doxa* that it would be risky to ignore. Let's take a look now at psychiatry to see if it is faring any better than the psychoanalysis whose cognitivisation it has masterminded.

CHAPTER FOUR

Cognitive-behavioural calculation*

> Are we really to allow our existence to be debased to the point of a servile exercise of calculation? Above all else, be sure not to seek to divest it of its ambiguous character.
>
> —F. Nietzsche, *The Gay Science*

Revolution

La Cousine Bette

The Revolution left such a mark on the minds of the fine country of France that in less than two decades the "insane" were being set apart from the common-law prisoners to whom previously they had been chained. Hitherto their suffering had been judged demoniac, but now at last it was to be secularised by a few doctors who dubbed it "mental illness" and then promptly appropriated it for themselves. Psychiatry

---

*This chapter and the one that follows were published in Issue 36 of the journal *La règle du jeu* (edited by B.-H. Lévy), as Aflalo, 2008b. They have been modified for the present edition.

was born. Freed of the supernatural, but also of the passions of the soul, the psychiatrists set about tracking down the secrets of human nature that for far too long had been deemed untreatable. Since its inception, however, psychiatry has harboured a gnawing bitterness, always feeling itself to be the impoverished little sister of medicine, scorned like Balzac's cousin Bette for its congenital lack of scientificity. If it is true that the microscope is scarcely of any help in studying madness, it is because madness is not a foreign body in human existence. It says what it is. Reason and unreason are spun with the same thread. Only the way the thread is knotted differs from person to person. So, as ever, freedom and madness are the speaking being's most loyal companions.

Determined to take vengeance on psychoanalysis for having been more swiftly ennobled than it would have liked, psychiatry, now won over to CBT and forgetful of *In Praise of Folly*, has wiped the slate clean of the enlightenment of the Freudian discovery, even though the latter was what fetched it out of the moralising rut into which the psychiatrists had thrust it in the first place. With its neonatal convulsions long behind it, but still tossed about by stormy seas, a handful of pro-CBT psychiatrists, barricaded behind their prejudices about insanity and anxious to play their small part at the university, whipped up a palace coup. Silent and slow to begin with, then sombre and fatal, but always faithful to the cunning spirit of revolutions, it soon came back to its point of departure to greet the deleterious return of "mental illness" and celebrate the splendid academic worth of the medical corporate body. And so, over the last quarter of the twentieth century, the revolution in psychiatry came to pass. The time for transparency was upon us and none would be allowed to resist.

Original sin

In an attempt to efface what certain academics thought was the original sin of psychiatry, they tried to force it into the fold of science. Next, they had us believe that to satisfy the scientific spirit the most intimate secrets would have to be misappropriated so as to bring the inexpressible part of human nature to yield. But the human being will not become an object of science, lest he lose his soul, that is to say, his mind and spirit, when put under study. So, having opted to navigate in the troubled waters of CBT, this would-be "mental science" sank to its darkest depths. The engineered collapse of cognitive psychoanalysis showed some of its hidden reefs, but the scuttling of psychiatry was the doing of academics who had consented to the spread of scientism and cognitive-behavioural assessment. In the space of a few years, the policy of issuing questionnaires had dismissed the clinic altogether.[1] With diagnostics now a statistical affair, each diagnosis is bitterly contested by a whole string of experts who impose a revision of the human condition that they would have submit to their diktat, giving vent to the potty idea that such a thing as "mental health" exists.

Being "put to the question"

The tests

These days it is hard to pick up a woman's magazine or a weekly that does not include some feature test or other promising to let you *know yourself better*, not to mention *your other half*. The question can be found splashed across the covers in one of a variety of forms: *Discover the hidden star in you, Do you know what he really wants?, What's your secret obsession?, What does it take to transport you to cloud 9?*, and whatnot. A dozen or so questions, sometimes more, tell you how to get to the bottom of the soul's mysteries, to unravel the puzzles of men, women and couples, and so on and so forth. To know who you really are, who your partner really is, what is wrong with your relationship and how to put it right, you just have to tick the boxes. The way you calculate the score depends on the magazine. More often than not, you tick a box on a short scale from one to six that will give you a series of numbers to tot up. Sometimes you pass first through a colour, a letter, or a sign that afterwards you convert into a score. Once you have your result, your Being is no longer impenetrable! Bingo, you've been evaluated! Though you might find this an amusing pastime, it is no laughing matter when it is used at the university to define your Being scientifically. And yet, this kind of test has become just as essential at the university as it is in such magazines. In these tests we meet what the supporters of CBT call "mental science".

The method

Academic research has been working flat out to go on churning out questionnaires that it pompously names "research tools". This obsessive, ritualised and uncontrollable practice of "the question" stands in for empirical scientific method. But the evils of empiricism are joined by the vices of CBT, with not one of their inventions actually managing to abide by the goal it was set: the observation of facts that exist solely in the present (i.e., mental symptoms) to be isolated for treatment. The scored answers of which the assessment is comprised replace quality with quantity, replace the description of phenomena with numerical figures, and are organised into complicated statistics that mask over the innate fault in knowledge. Bedecked with garlands of calculations, the mental symptoms step out in all their finery, imitating medical symptoms that lend themselves to numerical measure (for example, a fever that might have to be treated without a moment's delay).

The questionnaire method ensures that certain types of behaviour are observed, codified and quantified. In reality, they are reduced to lists of straightforward questions and given a numerical value, as in the magazine tests. The methodology amounts to nothing more than drawing up questionnaires which we are told consist in:

> [...] posing questions in the most objective manner possible and devising a protocol that, once implemented, will allow the individual to reply to these questions by selecting suitable measures. (Cottraux & Bouvard, 2005, p. 8)

By "protocol", we are to understand, "a stack of questions and questionnaires". As for the objectivity of the questions and the selection of the measures, let's take a look at what is involved.

The calculations

These objective questions are exclusively those designed by the CBT flunkies. They are put to use by infinitely carving up the symptoms that were erstwhile isolated by classical psychiatry (and then by psychoanalysis), and this has been done in such a way that there are now dozens of questionnaires for each new symptom that CBT has come up with. Indeed, to make the idea of the Freudian unconscious disappear, symptoms must henceforth be defined in terms of an accessible and utterly transparent knowledge. This is why symptoms are being first and foremost divested of their opacity of jouissance and the logical structure that can account for them. Next, they are being "dumbed down" to a simple and easily accessible term: panic, anxiety, social skills, OCD, stress, depression, psychotic disorders, sexual problems, relationship issues, etc. Once they have been submitted to the false evidence of the questions that presuppose a transparent knowledge accessible to consciousness, the subjects are considered to be the product of their answers, which are rapidly converted into numbers. This is how the calculations of evaluation intend to triumph.

For each questionnaire, the selection of "suitable" measures consists in applying a scoring system that also goes from one to six, depending on whether the given response is "not at all", "just a little", "quite a lot", "very much", etc. As you will have noticed, the principle behind this "quantification" is the same as that of "pick a number" paper fortune-tellers, only here, it is not about flirting, but doing away with the subject by passing from quality to quantity, from the appreciation of the subject to the computed result, in order to reach, so they believe, scientific objectivity. In reality, this is nothing but a sleight of hand where a number is put on a ticked box. The sum of figures is then statistically number crunched: this being the scientific guarantee of the whole enterprise for the naïve and the hurried.

As for the rest, who are harder to take in, the discourse of evaluation tries to lull them to sleep by speaking in learned tones: they don't say "tests dreamt up at one end of a kitchen table" but "research protocols established in academic laboratories". As for the rhetoric employed by the said academics, its monotony barely conceals its poverty.

The rhetoric

These questionnaires produce two kinds of assessment: self- and hetero-assessment. In the former, an "individual" (the patient) ticks boxes to evaluate himself; the latter are designed for the CBT technicians who tick the same boxes to "evaluate" the said individual. If the results do not concur, then a new calculation is necessary. This is known as the kappa coefficient. It sets an average or an "inter-rater agreement" that masks the subjectivity of the CBT technicians along with the subjectivity of those who have devised the scales and who are now lost to their sums. Thus, we can read in the CBT manuals that, "verifying the measuring tool is not the rule" (Cottraux & Bouvard, 2005, p. 3). The goal of this scientistic rhetoric is clear enough, but no conclusions are drawn from this avowal. Evaluation must continue to pass itself off as an exact science. Can we imagine a scientist saying that his method and his calculations are false, but carrying on and putting his name to them regardless? This is what the supporters of CBT are doing, with arguments that never vary: a first concession followed by the promise of imminent relief and you're all set! Let the farce continue! These rhetoricians have contaminated national and international institutions alike, including the World Health Organization. Indeed, the WHO applied their assessment principle when it created the ICD (*The International Classification of Diseases and Related Health Problems*), which rivals the North-American DSM (*The Diagnostic and Statistical Manual of Mental Disorders*). Needless to say, each of these classifications comes in very handy for conquering lucrative portions of the healthcare market.

The clinic dismissed

From bedside to bookshelf

The classical psychiatric clinic suffered from many flaws, but it was not lacking in finesse. Semiology was its specific area of expertise, and the doctor would visit his patient at his bedside to listen intently to his suffering. In France, in the wake of the events of May 1968, psychiatry's battle to gain recognition of its particularity culminated in its divorce from neurology. A specific internship was set up for those who wanted to specialise in the psyche, and students benefited from the wealth of lessons to be drawn from the French and German clinical traditions. Sometimes they might even come into contact with the Freudian discovery and Lacan's teaching at the university. Then, some ten years ago, a bill decreed the return of psychiatry to the fold of medicine, reverting to one sole internship for all medical disciplines and effectively sounding the death knell for such teaching. Psychiatry was cast into the lion's den of CBT evaluation. Since then, the supporters of the DSM have been putting on their academic dog and pony show, forcing it upon psychiatric wards so as to purge them of any who are hostile to its calculations. The result was not slow in coming: psychiatrists have become so few and far between that there is now a desperate shortage on the wards.

Established in the US under the leadership of the CBT flunkies who hold sway at the American Psychiatric Association, the DSM very quickly became a key reference throughout our western democracies. Some departments of university psychiatry that were favourable to cognitive-behavioural evaluation immediately took it on board without breathing a word, delighted at being able to seize the occasion to usurp the cloak of mathematical science by means of this statistical godsend and hopeful that the sham would go unnoticed.

The super market

The classifications in the DSM are produced using the same evaluative procedure. Next, they become the object of statistical calculations that are as complex as they are nugatory, but which have to impress the credulous and the financial backers. To persuade them of this, we cannot urge them strongly enough to read the books that Kirk and Kutchins have dedicated to this topic (Kirk & Kutchins, 1992, 1997). The critical analysis given by these two scientists demonstrates how the DSM has effectively decreed just about all types of behaviour a "mental disorder", without paying the slightest heed to public protest.

Rather than being a piece of scientific work, the DSM is more of a free market of diagnostics in the service of powerful economic interests, particularly pharmaceutical ones. This is no doubt what explains how psychiatry now stands as the only medical discipline for which the diagnoses are settled on the basis of the effect produced by the medication, rather than the real cause of the "illness". For example, antidepressants have given rise to the notion of "depression *per se*" which lumps together all the different causes of sadness to be met in neurosis and psychosis; likewise, sedatives for children have given rise to the notion of "hyperactivity" without identifying the multiple causality behind the agitation and anxiety that have simply continued to evolve. It would be hard to imagine the same thing in medicine. What kind of doctor would dare to label an entire heteroclite range of suffering with a term such as "heart disease", "liver disease" or "kidney disease", just because one type of medication had the power to mask the most evident manifestations of a cause that remained untreated? "Mental abnormality" is now a major market, and not only in the US.

The DSM has not given rise to any independent verification whatsoever. To this day, not a single study has contradicted the results obtained by Kirk and Kutchins and the way they called into question the reliability and validity of the statistics used in the manual. Are not such a lack of reliability and validity unacceptable in the field of science? The argument for "scientific validation" that is being spouted so vigorously by the defenders of CBT does not make it any less impossible to obtain. The evaluative procedure, which is never sufficiently accurate when it comes to isolating mental symptoms, goes on increasing the number of pages in the DSM without any clinical advance providing a justification for it. In these classifications, neither the subject nor the clinic of the case is ever invoked, only the consensus of psychiatrists.

The dictatorship of consensus

Theoretically speaking, psychiatrists have to apply the empirical method of the observation of symptoms in order to establish a diagnosis. In practice, indisputable psychical facts are being replaced with bitter discussions. It is not the facts themselves that are being taken into account, but consensus among experts, many of whom also have to satisfy the insurance firms they work for. In other words, for want of being able to *behold* the mental symptoms, the experts have been negotiating them, keeping only what they can agree on amongst themselves. In switching from the facts to the ideas that the "experts" have about those facts, science has given way to scientism.

The only thing at stake for the psychiatrists is agreement amongst themselves, but this can be no easy matter given what we know about the intensity of pressure exerted by certain groups who would like to see such and such a symptom included in or removed from the "super" market of diagnoses. In the US, for example, this so-called "empirical science" was made to withdraw any reference to the homosexualities. The rub is, it kept the heterosexualities. Wouldn't objectivity have implied that they too be withdrawn? Unless what lies at the very heart of mental symptoms is not, precisely, as we have already highlighted, sexuality itself, the impossible writing of man's Being, of woman's Being, necessarily missed and ever to be begun anew in symptoms.

CBT tries to impose the idea that mental *symptoms* are *disorders* and that these disorders have a threefold origin. First, they are alleged to be due to a learning error, but also to include biological and social components. This was how mental symptoms were transformed into "biopsychosocial" symptoms. Note that the dictatorship of consensus, with its disdain for the Real, was thereby setting out to lay down the law for mental symptoms. The pro-CBT universities have thus been condemning psychiatry to a "biopsychosocial" hell and finding fresh opportunity to lend support to a fear-mongering discourse that is clamoured all the more intently given that it is doomed to fail. Once the "experts" have negotiated the *mental symptoms* of international nomenclature, there will no longer be any need for a single practitioner to spend time with his patients. Patients will be hospitalised less and less (even when they need to be), and most of the time the diagnoses will be made in prison following the kinds of *passages à l'acte* we have seen hitting the headlines with ever-greater frequency. As a reaction to this, the very same university "experts" have been organising new meetings aimed at consensus decision-making so as to "acknowledge and take charge of" this clinic which remains resistant to questionnaires and from which they have cut themselves off definitively. This is the case, for example, with the consensus meetings on schizophrenia or "suicidal crisis". In the case of the latter, the title itself shows how the *passage à l'acte* has been disconnected from the clinic of the case and the neurotic or psychotic logic of subjects' symptoms. Which is why these consensus meetings amount to admissions of failure with respect to the empirical method of questionnaires. After cutting the heart out of the clinic of the subject, it no longer affords a way of grasping the logic behind *passages à l'acte*, and any possibility of prevention is doomed to fail. The point of such an enterprise may quite legitimately be called into question. I shall single out at least one vested interest: to make people believe that such a thing as a mental *norm* exists.

Mental health

A logical undecidable

How can mental health be defined scientifically? Let's be clear from the outset: it is impossible. This is why, strictly speaking, it has always been a misuse of language when psychiatry talks in terms of "mental illness". Illness implies the idea of recovery as a return to health. If recovery is the return to an initial normal state, how is this initial mental state to be defined? Who will judge it? And how? Medicine can objectively judge health because the real of the organism, which can be measured and computed, obeys the laws of science. For example, blood pressure or blood-sugar levels are real constants in the organism that cannot vary without triggering a cardiovascular illness, diabetes, or some such. But what constants could possibly define mental health? They do not exist. To claim the contrary by means of questionnaires is a sham. The real of the psyche, the mental real, is the jouissance of the speaking being. This jouissance may well be lawless, but it does have a cause. This means that instead of obeying the laws of science, it has a singular causality, one that is unique to each subject and cannot be converted into numerical figures or quantified. Do we really think that a box on a CBT questionnaire will keep up its illusion for long? For Lacan, who gave serious consideration to this question, the problem of defining mental health stems from a logical undecidable.

Moral assistance

If mental health eludes science, it is above all because the "mental" does not fall within its province. How is the "mental" defined? If we go by the dictionary, what is "mental" comes under the heading of the mind and its intellectual functions. It is the entirety of habits and beliefs that command thinking. It is also the state of mind, its psychological or moral disposition. Judgement, belief, and morality are intellectual faculties that stem from the freedom of thought. This freedom is incompatible with the strict determinism of science. As soon as it is a question of belief, we leave behind the arena of science. The "mental" may still be defined, but this definition cannot be a scientific one. The same holds true for mental "normality". It can be defined, but this "norm" will not be scientific either, it will be moral. Therefore, "mental health" is merely the sum of moral prejudices that govern the questionnaires. When considered from this angle, one can see that it rules out any freedom of thought, judgement, and decision-making on the part of the human being.

The unicorn and the centaur

Faced with this impasse, how did the CBT experts proceed? They concealed this impossibility by transforming mental health into a statistical concept. In this way, statistical reality will account for "mental" health. In other words, these empiricists have substituted calculations for the facts that stand to be observed. They have replaced the reality of facts with the reality of statistics, as if calculations were enough to make the reality of what has been calculated exist. But do statistics about unicorns make unicorns exist? We can agree on the number of limbs a centaur has, but it is by no means sure that such a consensus would make the centaur exist. Calculations on prejudices will change nothing of their intrinsic nature as prejudices. The average man only exists as the statistical fiction that we owe to Quételet (Quételet, 1969), and which Lacan denounced (Lacan, 2004). Canguilhem too rejected the concept of statistical reality. He did not recoil from making a critique of this slippery slope, including its definitions of the biological "norm", because he deemed that life is a concept of value and that medical judgement is not (Canguilhem, 1991). The keystone of the entire edifice rests upon the efficacy of belief in the existence of such a thing as "mental health". Without this belief, we would not have the calculations and the sliding they bring with them.

The slippery slope from the moral to the administrative

By replacing the mental with statistical calculus, the CBT technicians have replaced the object of study with its instrument. They have replaced the mental with the statistical, which is the means of study, and once this substitution has been accomplished, the Real of the mental has disappeared: it is no longer a matter of quality, but of quantity. This operation of reducing mental symptoms brings with it at least three slippery slopes.

The first slope leads from the normal to the normative. We have just seen that the *mental norm*, which is inaccessible to science, is always founded on a value judgement, that is to say, it comes under the heading of the moral.

The second slope leads from the mental to the organic. Using statistics allows conceptual tools to be pinned onto the mental; tools that are applicable to the organism. This operation stems from the materialist and reductionist theories that are currently dominant in the Anglo-American field. In the absence of any mental organ whose dysfunction would be valid in every case, a mental *norm* is devised using statistics that pass themselves off as a universal truth.

Lastly, the artifice of statistical calculus forces the passage from the pathological to the normal, from "mental illness" to "mental health". Here, the use of statistical calculus brings about a decisive semantic shift whereby the statistical mean becomes the statistical norm, and then the *norm* per se, to become, ultimately, *mental normality*.

Having admitted the idea that a mental and psychical norm exists, the supporters of CBT can claim that all those who fall wide of this norm do not simply *deviate* from the statistical average, but that they *are* deviant. "Deviant" is here to be understood as *carriers of mental illness in need of rehabilitation*. The outlandish category of "child hyperactivity" has been manufactured with methods such as these. But in the name of the "scientific principle" that truth cannot be heard from the mouth of a child, what the child says is no longer taken into account when he is assessed. Assessing those around the child, along with reports from CBT experts, will be enough to decree his abnormality. Here, the abjectness of the "norm" stretches to include getting mothers to consent to the consequences of their children's "abnormality": making them undergo CBT rehabilitation and take prescription medication. How long will it take for the consequences of this abuse to be spotted by the lawmakers and for them to take appropriate action to put an end to it, as is already the case in the US?

The DSM does not hide the fact that its diagnoses are constructed using statistical calculations. Moreover, the academic supporters of CBT have succeeded in imposing the same procedures on the WHO. Indeed, back in 1978, the WHO replaced the bothersome notion of "mental illness" with the equally problematic notion of "mental health" which it defines as "a state of complete physical, mental, and social well-being". Our condition as sexuated and mortal beings lies at the root of a good many forms of mental suffering. Could it ever be cured by the mere idea of well-being? And who could judge it to have been cured, if not the subject himself?

This kind of solution clearly consists in shifting the problem as in the famous adage *there is no problem that an absence of solution cannot solve*. With their cross-eyed vision which makes beings look like simple entities, sliding insidiously from the real to the fictive, from medicine to moralising, and from subversive doctrines to business, the supporters of CBT and their accomplices have set about launching an assault on the politicians, hoping to convince them to give legal backing to their doctrines.

Evaluating symptoms

The questionnaire method leaves no room whatsoever for the Freudian discovery. Considering symptoms as a fact of language that harbours a truth to be deciphered is therefore out of the question. They are transformed into an array of simplistic items that enable them to be evaluated. Once pared down into small units of behaviour or cognition, with the goal of reaching a constant signification that can be easily computed, they have effectively been reduced to a quantity in excess that stands to be corrected. This excessive quantity becomes an object of study and is classified as a monstrosity, just as one might classify a plant or an animal. Henceforth, transparency is required to make it accessible to the gloomiest of calculations. A few examples will give some idea of this cognitive-behavioural "science" and its relentless hunt for the enigma of the living, sexuated being. The old and the young, the psychotic and the non-psychotic: none escape its grasp. Let's take a closer look at what this yardstick is made of.

Life and death

How is one to evaluate "objectively" depression in the old or the very old? An evaluation scale with thirty or so questions professes to establish the diagnosis *scientifically*. Four of these questions will give us an idea of the suitability of the experts who have put together these tests: "Are you hopeful about the future?", "Do you worry about what will happen to you in the future?", "Are you afraid that something bad is going to happen to you?", "Is it hard for you to get started on new projects?". Do these questions really come from science? Don't they aim rather at drawing out a self-condemnatory spirit in our elders in the evening of their lives?

Childhood phobias are legion, so how is one to decide whether a child is really "phobic" or not? One of the rare questionnaires designed for children gives the impression that they are being treated no better than our veterans: *are you afraid of: going to the hospital; getting lost in a strange place; snakes; nasty dogs; wolves; spiders; going to the dentist; catching a serious illness; rats; being cut or hurt; your parents fighting; being burnt; going to the doctor's; getting an electric shock; graveyards* and so on. Isn't it precisely the consciousness of knowing oneself to be mortal that constitutes the dignity of humanity, from infancy onwards? Decidedly, it is not a good thing to be a child in the hands of a CBT technician.

A question of delusion

The questionnaires on "psychotic disorders" have to include a temporal element because on-the-spot observation is not sufficient when it comes to grasping psychotic symptoms. Now, for empiricism, observation must be strictly limited to what is discernible. Empiricism is thus caught out by the CBT evaluators themselves. Note too that these questionnaires do not gather the patient's replies but only those of the evaluators. Furthermore, these questionnaires only concern "individuals" who have been judged apt for social rehabilitation, the others being excluded from the outset. Wishing the other's well-being comes up against limits much earlier on in the process given the fact that the risks of failure (which are logged in the record books) would be compromising. Once the symptom's opacity has been dismissed, the subject is expected to know what makes him suffer and to tick with the greatest of ease the right box that corresponds to his "trouble". Neurotics do not know what makes them suffer, so are we seriously to imagine that a psychotic should know any more about it? Does a schizophrenic always know how to distinguish between reality and his hallucinations? Does a paranoiac know that he is delusional? Admittedly, expert consensus has removed paranoia from the international classifications, but is one honestly to believe that this is enough to stop it from existing? Could such a thing be entertained in medicine? Does a myocardial infarction cease to exist just because a group of cardiologic experts says so?

Sexuality

CBT experts came up with the diagnosis "social phobia" to transform shyness and reserve into an illness. The form the questionnaires take gives some idea of this: *Do you avoid or are you anxious about: telephoning people you don't know well; meeting new people; meeting the opposite sex; organising get-togethers?* Once again, isn't this more about getting a word of avowal from one's most private intimacy, an avowal about the encounter with the opposite sex which is always fraught and problematic? Hunting out such an avowal reinforces the discontent that our society of the spectacle generates through its forced exhibitionism.

The questionnaires dedicated to "sexual problems and couples issues" are no different from those found in the magazines. They are supported by the idea that the Being of man or the Being of woman is something that can be known and written down. CBT mysticism mixes up the writing of the sexual relation with sexual intercourse (which it thinks of as something "harmonious" and whose jouissance could be quantified). The couple it envisages is here defined as necessarily heterosexual and legitimate. Thus, a *curriculum vitae* of the couple quantifies the understanding between the two partners with the aid of nine questions on their budgeting, their good manners, their philosophy of life and, of course, their relations with the in-laws. What a strange science this is whose observation deprives humans of the fire and passion of love and desire, not to mention the paradoxes of jouissance.

OCD

The questionnaires for "obsessive compulsive disorder" are not without interest either. We can gain some understanding of how they work by looking at the way they treat the dimension of time and the dimension of truth. First of all, observation limited to on-the-spot thought and behaviour is, of course, insufficient. It has to include the past. Once again, the experimental method that requires observation of real-time facts is invalidated, and once again the pretension of scientific objectivity is maintained. Moreover, we may note that observation submitted to a standardised limit yields to what is arbitrarily apportioned by the clock. Bergson was condemning this deception back in 1912 in his lecture on "The mind and the body". More recently, the idea that science brings about a *foreclosure of time* was formalised by Jacques-Alain Miller in a way that allows for its logic to be grasped (Miller, 2001a, pp. 8–36). No arbitrary apportioning of time by science will ever account for the peculiar temporality of the relation to jouissance. As soon as symptoms are at issue, the practice of questionnaires necessarily comes up against the problem of time. The idea that symptoms are an incessant repetition certainly crosses the minds of the partisans of CBT, but taking this on board would immediately disqualify their method and bring down the whole edifice.

Next, the practice of questionnaires comes up against the truth it represses. Truth has no place in the disorder the experts have devised, but having been excluded, it is constantly returning in their obsession with exactitude, which can be read in the way they hunt out the lie in the one who is being put to the question. They spend a considerable amount of time coming up with questionnaires that they never deem sufficiently accurate. Therefore they are constantly forced to include new lists of questions to supplement the old questionnaires and verify the exactitude of the replies that have been given. More often than not, two-dozen questions is enough for them to produce a diagnosis, but to diagnose OCD, they need a hundred or so. Here are two such questions: "Do you feel the excessive need to check things?" and "Do you engage in excessive list-making?" Don't say you haven't been warned!

Lie-telling is just one of many examples that stigmatise first "individuals" and then whole "populations". The supporters of CBT deem the statement that some populations tell lies more than others (for example the French in comparison with the English) to be "scientific". No doubt prudence dictates that one should not bite the hand that feeds. What holds our attention here is less the casual manner with which the Epimenides paradox is swept aside in order to discredit the French exception, than the application of such stigmatisation to whole "populations" and then to entire nations.

These few examples give some insight into the ravaging moralism that governs the CBT version of symptoms carved into chunks. Their unproven novelty comes up against such a degree of inefficacy that the manufacture of further questionnaires becomes necessary so as to mask over this state of affairs. And now we have questionnaires for personality too.

Evaluating personality

The heart of the symptom

Being inexpressible, what lies at the heart of symptoms cannot feature on any type of questionnaire. Firmly ignoring this structural fact, the CBT specialists hope to remedy it by inventing their own questionnaires, and university research labs are now teeming with them. Establishing lists of *symptoms*, that is to say, "observable faults in behaviour and thinking", always runs aground when it comes to questions related to the living, sexuated being. The inefficacy of this manufacture of symptoms has driven the "experts" to invent yet more of them, which they term "personality disorders". They can now justify the unpleasant aftertaste they leave: if the disorders (which they themselves have cut to measure) resist their treatments, then the personality of the "individual" must be incriminated (and not their method). The advantage of this is clear: given the inefficacy of carving up mental symptoms into chunks, the cause is now to be imputed to the personality which is deemed to be inaccessible to change. Case made.

Forgetting Sade

The task of this new evaluation is shared between psychiatrists and psychologists: the former manufacture the deviations of the personality, the latter quantify them. These new questionnaires have seen violent debates among the experts. They agree on nothing, neither the nature of the "facts" of the supposed deviation, nor the number of them (which varies between one and ten). Once again, the consensual solution must prevail. This does not even concern the observation of facts anymore, but only their number, set at five without anyone really knowing why. This "factor five" then becomes the most crucial element: the "Big Five" (also known as OCEAN, which lives up to its name with its immense, limitless drifting).

For our learned experts, the personality stems from socio-biology. Manufacturing this chimera allows the deadlock to be displaced. Their theory holds that behaviour can always be rehabilitated, but in practice this has ended in widespread failure. Thereafter, *personality* is called into question. Being a genetic and environmental affair, it is less malleable, but to displace the problem is not to solve the problem, far from it. The paradox of jouissance is lost on the pastoral vision of evaluation which only takes on board the Kantian side of happiness (as a function of morality) and eliminates the singular side, that is, the Sadean aspect of *happiness in evil* which has been bothering thinkers down through the centuries. CBT runs aground on the problem of the persistence of symptoms and the "deviant personalities" that are resistant to the awards given in recompense for normalising them or making them disappear. Thorndike was already coming up against this problem in the first half of the twentieth century.[2] But how is one to account for the persistence of undesirable conduct and its catastrophic consequences for the subject without taking into account the death drive (*cf.* Aflalo, 1996)?

The cognitive-behavioural therapies

It is worthwhile recalling that the "cognitivism" of CBT has very little to do with the current of thought that bears the same name. The cognitivism that CBT claims for itself is more of a theoretical patchwork that imparts the vague allure of a science.

Reductive principles

The cognitive-behavioural therapies are a direct application of the academic research we mentioned above. They are shot through with such a high degree of heterogeneity that one would be hard pushed to define the principle that would make a natural science of all this. Indeed, the advocates of behaviourism and the advocates of cognitivism do not even share the same conception of human nature. For behaviourists, man and animal are identical, since there is no difference between the adaptability of man's behaviour and that of the laboratory rat. On the other hand, for the CBT-cognitivists, the human being is identified with one of his organs, the brain, which is itself reduced to computer processing. The two projects are thus fundamentally opposed. For behaviourists, the human being is merely the sum of his various types of behaviour; for the CBT-cognitivists, he is merely the sum of various computer programmes. For the former, there is merely an organism; for the latter, there is merely language, but language reduced to a code. These two currents succeeded one another in time, but ultimately formed an alliance. One thing made this unnatural union of chalk and cheese possible: they both reject the human being as a being of speech. Their reductionist approach allows them to affirm that the psyche obeys the organism's determinism alone, and that therefore it is governed by scientific laws. Regardless of the ideal at stake, whether the ethology of the behaviourist or the artificial machine of the would-be cognitivist, it will always boil down to denying the dignity of the speaking being and the truth of his complaint. From these very same reductive principles, poorly made over at that, the CBT "experts" have deduced treatments to be applied to the human being which are now commonly known under the name "cognitive-behavioural therapy".

Therapeutic education

These therapies are standardised, methodical training techniques reputed for their brevity. Two examples will afford us a taste of this. Our first case is a woman who suffers from acute panic attacks, particularly when she opens her mail. For the supporters of CBT, the *successful treatment* of panic attacks consists in re-educating her by means of authoritarian conditioning in such a way that in a few sessions' time she will be calmly opening her letters. From this angle, her anxiety is never considered to be the sign of a Real that has to be taken seriously. This is why the Real goes on making itself felt, but differently, through the displacement and reinforcement of her anxiety, either in the extension of her inhibition or in the formation of further symptoms. One self-same logic is at work across inhibition, anxiety, and symptoms. Freud demonstrated this quite well enough. To mask their failures, the fervent supporters of CBT prefer to ignore this unit and to carve symptoms up into multiple items, along with their corollaries of anxiety and inhibition. They do this so completely that the bonds and displacements between symptoms, anxiety, and inhibition are also deliberately ignored. They then try to have us believe that authoritarianism is enough to make them disappear. If the argument for authority could really hold such sway over the symptomatic malaise that dwells within us from our earliest years on, this would surely have been recognised by now. It is precisely because symptoms have an unconscious cause that the argument for authority will never win through. One can break in a horse, but the dignity of man objects to this kind of training.

In our second case, a psychotic patient is considered to have been successfully treated when he manages to conceal his suffering (Cottraux & Blackburn, 2001, p. 126). That concealment should be considered a *scientifically valid* treatment will raise a few eyebrows, not just for those in the profession. Note that in both cases, CBT is said to be efficient and its statistics will record positive results in the assessment of the treatment's efficacy.

The educational therapists qualify themselves as educationalists. They apply methods that were founded on conditioned reflexes, perfected on Pavlov's dogs, and put to the test by Skinner. The conditions may vary, ranging from the most simple to the most sophisticated, from auto-suggestion right through to fierce dissuasion. What takes place is thus referred to as "interaction between the therapist and the individual or 'learner'."

The benefits of treatment

This pedagogy calls itself democratic because it functions on the basis of a "therapeutic contract for self-management". It has to be brief in order to be profitable. The partial effectiveness of these methods is not to be doubted because it is the efficacy of suggestion. Having excluded both truth and the real, however, this efficacy is limited. "Thought-stopping" treatment for obsessions demonstrates the failure of this: the obsessional thoughts simply will not stop. If suggestion does manage to sweep away a few of them, others take their place, and they will be just as invasive and may even multiply. Indeed, psychoanalysis teaches us that a symptom can be modified in the long term if and only if one gets to its unconscious cause.

Another benefit is to be derived from these educational treatments. The implicit goal is to master the subject's jouissance. Sometimes this goal becomes explicit as with the "aversive" procedures that aim to cure the patient by methodically anguishing him. For example, a young child suffering from arachnophobia will be put in contact with spiders, in spite of his fears, until the anxiety subsides. This will go on until his complaint comes to an end. Is it not the case that the sadistic fantasies of the therapists that were already showing through in the questionnaires find even greater satisfaction in the execution of these treatments?

We are alluding to precise events here. John B. Watson, one of the first behaviourists, stirred up a chorus of indignation in the US when he brought on an experimental fright in an eleven-month-old baby (The Little Albert Study). More recently, CBT has reintroduced electric shock "treatments" which are being brought into general use for the most vulnerable subjects, in particular those deemed "mentally defective" who are resistant to CBT conditioning. A series of articles published in the *Encyclopédie médico-chirurgicale de psychiatrie* vouches for this (Miremont et al., 1990; Mirabel-Sarron & Vera, 1997; Dazord, 1997; Légeron & Van Rillaer, 1999; Cottraux, 2000). Contributions from psychoanalysis had nevertheless led such treatment to be banned or at the very least limited to very exceptional cases. They would never be prescribed as a first line of treatment. Today, however, on certain university psychiatric wards, it is no longer rare for them to be applied after the very first triggering of a psychosis, including for young women who have just given birth. Neuroleptics, which are generally not so harsh and tend to be more efficient, could at least be tried before embarking on this course of treatment. The mother–child relationship could only stand to gain from it. Be that as it may, whichever way one tries to "break in" the human being, it will never put an end to a symptom, not even in the form of these rather barbaric conditioning procedures that usurp the name "treatment" and fly in the face of the Hippocratic oath.

An OCEAN of false science

Freud began his work standing shoulder to shoulder with scientists, and he condemned their hypocrisy for refusing to acknowledge the sexual cause of the neuroses and psychoses. Their power is no less today than it was then. In certain universities and trusts, they want to make us believe that Freud's name lives on today solely by virtue of his physicalist interest in eels. The Lacanian formulation of the university discourse can shed light on the logic at work here: a pretension to govern based on knowledge that is conceived of as a totality. We have seen how this false knowledge renders the symptom unrecognisable. We shall add two further remarks:

1. The questionnaire with its tick boxes is a parody of knowledge. It brings onto the stage a kind of puppet-like *subject supposed to know* who would be objective, even though such a thing is impossible because the watchwords that organise one's destiny are peculiar to each subject. Furthermore, the unconscious is not only a knowledge. It also carries with it a belief whose modalities differ in the neuroses and the psychoses. The logical problems raised by beliefs (*qualia*) show that no list of questions, regardless of its length, will ever manage to objectify the *subject supposed to know*. Objections from the likes of Paul Churchland carry little weight faced with Hilary Putnam's critique of the metaphor of the "computer" brain which shows that the only thing to be got out of it is what was put there in the first place.
2. The use of numerical figures, which is just as contestable, pursues a twofold goal. First, that of leading the speaking being back to his "natural" state by making him believe that he is written in mathematical language, like nature. This will to reduce all that is human to a numerical knowledge constitutes a rectification of Being. It holds that two things that are numerically identical must share the same properties. But doesn't this amount to a misuse of Leibniz's principle on the identity of indiscernibles? Second, the use of numerical figures is merely a hopeless attempt to align jouissance as a whole with the signifier that counts and records it in the account books. For every human being, jouissance is the kernel of Being that stands "far away, so close", eluding the signifier and knowledge. To claim the contrary, or to have people believe as much, stems from a delusion that has harmful consequences when it takes control and sets out to regulate the "mental health" of private life.

The contemporary discontent

Evaluation is now one of the names for the discontent in our civilisation. It is no longer a matter of nostalgia for the father figure (with its corollary of repression as a limit to the jouissance of the drive), as it was in Freud's time (Freud, 1930a). Today's discontent stems from the invasion of objects that science has brought us. These objects range from the most throwaway knick-knacks to the most sophisticated gadgets that try to kid the economy of human jouissance. Human beings will not escape this mechanical future, nor will they elude the programmed destiny of *restitutio ad integrum*. This illusory promise of restoration is what stands in for a definition of mental and psychical health. The knowledge of science has already produced the theoretical scientism of CBT and the widespread commerce of its therapy. It will soon be producing a supermarket of organs and clones of every which type. Whether we are aware of it or not, and regardless of whether we actually want it, the body and "mental" health have already been put on the open marketplace. Therefore, they must yield to the laws of the market, to supply and demand, and to the imperative for profitability. Today, "mental" health has become a political factor. It would thus be useful to look more closely at the implications of this.

In conformity with the logic of the university discourse, when knowledge is at the helm it arbitrates the hidden will to master the peculiar jouissance of the subject. This is the logic of governing by means of the specific knowledge of "experts" in evaluation. It aims at extorting the evaluated subject's auto-critique. Today, the subject is being commanded to assent to the abjectness of voluntary servitude as required by evaluation. We may quite rightfully qualify this method as perverse. Wasn't this already legible in the countless questionnaires and treatments being proffered by CBT?

Its principle (i.e., what is put first) is just another way of finding the rabbit in the top hat, provided it was put there in the first place. The CBT methods and principles are an ocean of false science. Under the allure of statistics, however, the fantasy that steers it is what gives the greatest cause for concern.

The experience of one's own analysis allows those that so desire to grasp for themselves the perspective of their fantasy, so as to consent to be relieved of a major portion of their jouissance, and then to hold themselves responsible for what remains. We might also call to mind how some currents of thought have sought to build a rational critique of psychoanalysis. This is why, as a psychiatrist and a psychoanalyst, I am beset by a sense of shame faced with the wrongdoing perpetrated by colleagues who have let themselves be taken in by this deleterious science. This slippery slope has nothing ineluctable about it. To resign oneself to it is to participate in the furthering of its tyranny. We know very well that it only prospers when we give in to it one by one. And so the idea of the norm, so sadly celebrated, must be fought, methodically, in precisely those zones that concern the psyche.

CHAPTER FIVE

Discipline and banish

In the space of a few days, the fatalities multiplied and it become obvious to all who were grappling with this strange evil that a true epidemic had set in.

—A. Camus, *The Plague*

An epidemic at the university

The epidemic of evaluation, fostered by the supporters of CBT, has contaminated the university and nothing would seem to be capable of halting its spread. If we were to examine the particularities of this epidemic, what determines it and how it is distributed, we might form a grasp of its logic, and maybe even prevent it. To spell it right out: we would be doing a little epidemiology.

Epidemiology played a decisive role in the evolution of medical science. One discovery in particular affords some idea of its importance. Ignaz Philipp Semmelweis, a Viennese doctor and a contemporary of Freud, stopped a fatal epidemic of childbed fever that was decimating women who gave birth in hospital (and, crucially, *only* those who gave birth in hospital). Dr Semmelweis showed that their infection was caused by bacteria from corpses dissected by medical staff who passed from the autopsy room to the delivery room without washing their hands, thereby infecting their patients with a fatal septicaemia. This illness disappeared when Semmelweis managed, not without resistance, to get the doctors to wash their hands before examining their patients. Since then, antibiotics have made a great many more infections disappear. Epidemiology consolidated this triumph by adding prevention through hygiene. Associated with the other victories over the grim reaper that the last century saw, it enjoyed great renown.

Today, however, epidemiology is meeting serious difficulties. It is no longer managing to abate the new "nosocomial diseases" (hospital-acquired infections). In their determination to put an end to these fatal epidemics cultivated at the hospital, the bureaucrats have been putting hospital staff to work devising protocols of evaluation that are both sophisticated and onerous, cutting heavily into the time staff can spend with their patients, so much so that they no longer have time to spare on an adequate asepsis when they go from one patient to the next. Now that millions have been spent on their learned evaluations, the higher authorities in the ANAES (the Agence nationale d'accréditation et d'évaluation en santé)—since replaced by the HAS (Haute autorité de santé)—have been summoning medical staff to important meetings and recommending, as the preventive measure, that they wash their hands. It would seem that, since Semmelweis and his discoveries, epidemiology has not come up with anything else with which to combat fatal hospital-acquired infections besides evaluation.

Epidemiology looks to have been overrun on its native soil, so how are we to account for its colonisation of psychiatry? What germs does it have to protect itself against there? What microbes does it have to wash off its hands?

Infection of mental illnesses

Until the discovery and introduction of antibiotics midway through the last century, syphilis inspired as much dread as the white death (more widely known as tuberculosis). Its slow evolution, all the more frightful given that the illness enters unperceived, could culminate in a picture of dementia that leaves a lasting impression on anyone who has ever contemplated the spectacle. What was then termed "latent", "torpid" or "tuberculous" psychosis did a good job of mimicking the harrowing characteristics of genuine psychosis. It was not uncommon for poor demented souls infected with *treponema pallidum* or Koch's bacillus to wind up in asylums, shoulder to shoulder with outlaws and crooks, beggars and the needy, bewitched troublemakers, sorcerers, and others racked with hallucinations.

From the time of Esquirol (a pupil of the great Pinel who freed the insane from their chains), passing via Morel and on up to the pupils of the illustrious Kraepelin, all psychiatrists thought about "mental illness" using the model of syphilitic infection. However, they quickly added to this infectious model a supplementary complication that sought to vouch for the might of their knowledge (which nevertheless remained obscure to ordinary mortals): mental infection transmitted from one generation to the next. In short, they turned mental illness into a hereditary defect. It will come as no surprise, therefore, to learn that one of them came up with the idea of curing evil with evil and infecting some of these unfortunate souls (if they found themselves in range of his diagnosis and therapeutic arsenal) with malaria. This contemporary of Freud received the Nobel Prize for his noble invention. Allowing his name to fall from memory will be an act of charity.

In the interest of equality, the psychiatrists applied the infectious cause to everything they had labelled "mental illness": circular insanity, paranoia and schizophrenia, hysterical madness and childbed insanity, obsessions and phobias, the anomalies of psychopaths with homosexual tendencies, sadism and masochism, the mental anomalies of liars and crooks, pathological criminals and vagabonds, imbeciles, idiots, cretins, and such. They promptly deduced new classifications of simple-minded treatments based on good clean living. They believed that prohibiting people from frequenting dens of iniquity would prevent syphilis, as if female inconstancy and male infidelity—which were largely sufficient for the spread of the epidemic—could peter out along with vice and corruption, whilst desire, finally divorced from sin, could give the lie to the Scriptures. As for warding off the appalling effects of tuberculosis, it was a matter of combating a causal agent that was just as determined to slip away from the inquisitive eye of the scientist as it was eager to allow itself to be fostered by the misery the industrial age was relentlessly intensifying. This misery persisted in spite of the charities that started popping up; charities that successfully campaigned for the installation of free clinics up and down the country in the fight against tuberculosis and syphilis. The psychiatrists then found their place in these centres, renaming them "mental hygiene clinics" with the discovery of penicillin, since a few tablets were, indeed, all it took to be swiftly cured of each of these would-be hereditary defects, to the point that the clinics soon become deserted and useless. Aside from the universities, psychiatrists who work in the public sector are still housed in these premises today.

Thanks to the subtle and methodical work of Bentham, Great Britain was able to give itself hygiene laws that did not depend on goodness of heart and benefit societies. Hygiene having earned its science stripes just as the Eiffel tower was reaching to the sky, the first International Sanitary Conference, held in Paris, strove without success to codify the struggle against epidemics by means of less antiquated measures than quarantine and fire-cleansing. When the US finally agreed to commit, however, they still had to wait for the eleventh congress in the first days of the twentieth century to see the creation of the International Office of Public Health, which went on to become the League of Nations Health Organization, and then, in 1948, the WHO.

Alas, prejudices die hard, and science has little say in the matter. Our learned psychiatrists have had to capitulate on fire-cleansing and quarantine for their patients, but preoccupied as they have been with their posts at the university, they are still attached to the same beliefs as their elders. Determined to serve the same faith in sanitary moralising, they uphold, like their predecessors, the organic cause of "mental illness", though not without renaming it on the way with the tricky term "mental disorder". Yesterday's hereditary degeneration, hastily painted over with the colours of today's genetics, can thus remain intact as an organic cause that is affirmed all the more forcefully given that it still remains just as recalcitrant to the scientific demonstration we have been led to expect for decades now.

When he invented psychoanalysis, Freud criticised the psychiatric prejudices of his contemporaries, which in his view were designed to confirm the puritanical moralising of the hygienists. Indeed, how can one forget their devastating effects on patients and their posterity, as the case of Präsident Schreber bears out? We are forced to admit that the Freudian critique has lost nothing of its cutting edge. Having rallied for a while to the splendour of the worship of Reason, clarified by psychoanalysis but scarcely favourable to the hygienists, the psychiatrists soon turned back to their idols and the cult of goddess Hygieia. They decided to assure themselves of its benefits by means of a few propitiatory rites with the aid of questionnaires and statistics that were supposed to help them to eradicate the principle of evil and to conquer, or so they believed, with the same weapons that had stamped out the white death, the mental plague they judged to be just as purulent and insane.

The plague of mental health

In the age of science, the university has begat some of its finest beasts. The Loch Ness monster no longer brings in the money when the "mental health" monster is on the scene. By forcing the powers that be—first the WHO and then the lawmakers—to adopt its creature, the evaluators at the university knew they were going to get rich off the back of a weapon that is more powerful and more dissuasive than any of those they previously had at their disposal in their therapeutic arsenal. In 1978, the WHO's decision to switch from "mental illness" to "mental health" reconfigured the field of modern psychiatry by drafting in the battalion of epidemiology. The reign of the psychiatrists was finally upon us. From now on, the exercise of their power would no longer be limited to a few poor "mentally ill" asylum inmates. They were finally going to be allowed to exercise their talents on entire nations (who otherwise are in fairly good shape). Epidemiology in mental health, the new recruit in academic psychiatry, is just twenty-five years old. However, it is warmongering on the same national and international battlefields as psychiatry, and joins it in spreading the religious practice of mental health and belief in mental illness infection. Its preventive model stems from this.

For infectious illnesses, medical science taught three-phase prevention control. The first phase of preventive medicine (primary prevention) consists in isolating the infectious agent: the virus or bacterium. The second phase (secondary prevention) has to impede the evolution of the illness by prescribing *ad hoc* treatment—antibiotics, for instance. In the third phase (tertiary prevention), it has to prevent relapses and to limit any disabling after-effects. It is true that the observable symptoms of an epidemic are clearly defined in space and time. The infectious agent obeys the principle of strict causality. Contagion spreads in accordance with a law that can be defined scientifically. This is a field of medical science. We may add that the prevention of infectious risk falls to the public authorities. It includes the doctor's legal obligation to declare each case of life-threatening infectious disease. The same goes for well-known and age-old diseases like the plague and cholera, typhoid and smallpox, but also new forms of pestilence.

The epidemiology of organic illnesses functioned so well that it inspired academic psychiatrists contaminated by evaluation to create and classify their new "mental illnesses". They can be found in the DSM that serves as their handbook, which is cited at every opportunity but which is far too unwieldy to be useful to clinicians.

Civic illness

Metaphor driven out of the university

Just before the French Revolution, 1770 to be precise, the term "epidemic" took on a new metaphorical meaning: in French, one speaks of an *épidémie d'esprit* to designate "something that touches a large number of people by spreading *like* an epidemic."[1] Since then, we have used the term "contagion" to refer to widespread infatuation or fads, for instance an epidemic of violence, of xenophobia or of racism. In his "Second dialogue", Rousseau wrote: "there exist, so to speak, epidemics of the mind that spread from man to man like a kind of contagion."

It is in this metaphorical sense that people might speak of an epidemic of suicides. If the suicide of Empedocles has left such an indelible mark in our minds, isn't it because it testifies to the free causality of the subject? The number of those that have followed, whether enlightened or not, changes nothing. Freud was also employing the term metaphorically when he spoke of "hysterical epidemics". A girl in a boarding school breaks into tears after receiving a letter that brings an end to her relationship with a young man, whereupon the contagious sadness sweeps over all the other girls who had secretly been wishing to share her destiny and know something of the ways of love. Once again, the hysterics were the ones who indicated to Freud one of the secrets of the metaphor of the mental symptom: unconscious desire as the base of identification and its correlate of jouissance that affects the body. Without the mainspring of the intellectual faculties of judgement and belief, how can we speak of epidemics of the mind that embrace even the most determined fanaticism?

Metaphor, immortalised by Jakobson and given fresh practical implications by Lacan, was already known to Aristotle. It was Aristotle's teaching, as taken up by the Church Fathers, that laid the foundations of the university. When exactly was metaphor driven out of the university? It is hard to say with great accuracy. It is, however, possible to deduce retroactively the very moment at which evaluation moved in to its quarters. Psychiatrists won over to the delusion of evaluation used the expression "epidemic of the mind" not in a figurative way, but quite literally. Emboldened by this recent (re)discovery, and tooled up with scalpel and microscope, they quickly set about conducting postmortem examinations on the brains of suicide victims with a view to perfecting their preventive measures. The interest of this research was admittedly a bit late coming for the deceased, but not so for the psychiatrists. They refused to abjure their faith in the hereditary defects at the root of mental illnesses and went on hunting out the culprit gene that lay behind the lethal secretions that cunning doses of biomarkers would surely isolate some day. They clung to the mad hope of finally seeing through the lens of a microscope the root of evil that had eaten away at the victim's mind. Their obsolete research took on new vigour, as sudden as it was costly, but quite powerless to curb the rising number of suicide bombers. How could it be otherwise with such outlandish ideas? That said, the venerable Inserm did not hesitate to adopt these ideas as its own (Inserm Collective, 2005b). We can see here how one goes about the systematic destruction of knowledge in times of peace. Two conclusions may be drawn from this: first, that the discontent is being fostered at the university; second, that serious healthcare catastrophes are in store if we do not grasp in time what is at stake for public health.

Sociopathy

Alas, so long as it has not managed to isolate the microbes behind mental *disorders*, epidemiology is incapable of implementing any primary prevention strategies in mental healthcare. For the same reason, the vaccine that would immunise against mental disorders remains wishful thinking, compromising its public service mission of maintaining mental order (Lalonde, Aubut, & Grunberg, 1999). Moreover, this is precisely what psychiatrists are always being reproached for: they do not have a predictive science that would be efficient enough to know in advance the zero hour or the D-day when "mental disorders" break out.

In the twentieth century, dramatic industrialisation certainly polluted air, water, ground, and food, but given its benefits, preserving health from the crowd of misfits that industrialisation produced became a pressing concern. In opening up to globalisation, the technological age has also demanded social adaptation of *individuals*. Its increasingly rapid escalation means, however, that the heavy task of "mental adaptation" that now falls to psychiatrists is also mounting. One can thus understand epidemiology's zealous rush to make us forget its unfortunate powerlessness by efficiently attending to secondary and tertiary prevention.

Academic psychiatry, now renamed biopsychosocial psychiatry, has more than one number in the bag of tricks from which it draws (encountering not the least opposition) the alibis that will exonerate its young recruit *epidemiology* and save it from its innate futility. "Mental disorders" may well remain beyond the reach of biology, but they do not fall wide of the social realm. Pro-CBT academics have taken care to label social disorders "mental disorders" by saddling them with clever names like "antisocial personality disorder" (DSM-IV) and "dissocial personality disorder" (ICD 10). Secondary mental health prevention has thus become a major stake in public health, demanding that each nation be protected from "sociopathy" and these "socioheads" (to use the fine term coined by Philippe Sollers).

The cook, the politician, and the jobseeker

Tertiary prevention will have to insure that these agents—troublemakers who can be easily observed with the naked eye—do not give rise to an overly frequent return of social disorder (which always bodes ill for mental health) and that the social repercussions such disorder leaves behind do not spread inopportunely from individual houses to neighbourhoods and then to the nation as a whole.

As you will have grasped, epidemiology in mental healthcare is carrying out its public service in drawing on the principles and methods of CBT. As in CBT, it detects deviations from the norm by means of questionnaires and statistics. This is how its tertiary prevention has come to benefit from their rich invention: "rehabilitation in social and professional life". For the novices, we can specify that this is a matter of "empowerment" that leads towards a "normal life" by conforming to social norms. We owe this to Alain Braconnier:[2] "whether it is a matter of mixing a hollandaise sauce or trying to solve the Yugoslavia crisis, if inefficacy persists it triggers a highly characteristic chain reaction [...] [that goes] from learned helplessness to resignation." He goes on to explain that:

> [...] this phase is common to all persistent situations of failure: laboratory dogs on the receiving end of electric shocks and the long-term unemployed alike. A long-term jobseeker would thus pose a problem of "learnt helplessness", the first sign of a mental disorder to be corrected by ad hoc re-education. (Braconnier, 2001, pp. 70–71)

This political, social, and culinary analysis deserves to be appreciated for what it is worth. When the scourge of unemployment is at issue, once its causal factor of poor conditioning has been elucidated, are the jobless to be cured by means of treatment akin to that used on Pavlov's dogs: a good dose of mental health conditioning? Does ensuring well-being entail the widespread implementation of this procedure so that it will include the cook, the politician, and then the citizen at large? The academics who inspired the Accoyer Amendment upheld an analogous logic when they claimed to be "protecting the users", which did not escape the notice of Catherine Clément when she wrote: "Spread the net and survey. Punish politically. Protect the ill. Make no mistake, there are no more citizens, we are all ill now" (Clément, 2003).

To carry through this enterprise of averting biopsychosocial disorders, the epidemiologists have at their disposal considerable economic and moral resources, and their colleagues in medicine and law are providing them with useful support. The dreams of the evaluators at the university lacked neither ambition nor pretension, but they were still bound to remain precarious so long as they had not been legitimated in legal terms.

The French exception

The Amendment

As we have seen in our chronicle of the events surrounding the Accoyer Amendment, the Cléry-Melin roadmap went unnoticed. It was the Amendment itself that set the cat amongst the pigeons. The concurrence of these two intentions was explosive because the Cléry-Melin report was to serve as the blueprint for the Mental Healthcare Plan. Professor Wartel's reading of this was quite clear enough (Wartel, 2004): authoritarianism in mental health matters had every reason to worry us because it was being entrusted to the psychiatrists. They alone would be the ones to decide which shrink any given citizen would have to consult. It sometimes happens that the passing of certain laws arouses the anger of the public that they are supposed to protect. Such was the case with this amendment. It sought to close a legal loophole and provide security for patients by setting up a diploma for psychotherapists. The intention was commendable, but the consequence troubling. Coupled with the Cléry-Melin roadmap, the amendment amounted to a promulgation of state psychotherapy. This sort of procedure was common practice in the notorious totalitarian regimes, but never had a democratic state shouldered its way in betwixt patient and therapist. Every citizen is free to choose whomsoever he wishes to consult, and the state has neither the right to interfere in this choice, nor the right to contradict it. The ensuing events showed how legislators had been taken in by a clique of academics won over to CBT who wanted to outlaw Lacanian psychoanalysis. To decrypt the ins and outs of this strategy orchestrated behind the scenes, it will be useful to give a close reading of a few particular publications.

The Cléry-Melin report was signed by two other authors: Dr Kovess and Dr Pascal. Dr Kovess is a specialist in mental health epidemiology in France. She was invited by Jacques-Alain Miller to the first of the Forums, and she didn't fail to rise to the challenge and engage in honest debate. She is not lacking in flair, and I admit that I owe to her the little I know of her discipline. Without the Cléry-Melin report that pushed her name to the fore, I doubt I would ever have had the leisure time to read the manuals she has written or co-authored, and her discipline would still be quite foreign to me. In the medical bookshops I visited with an eye to learning something about CBT, her name caught my attention. I purchased two of her books that are still in print (Kovess, 1996; Kovess, 2001). Skimming through the first, I came across the signature of the eminent academic who prefaced it: D. Widlöcher. Several of her articles on epidemiology and alcohol prevention are cited as solid references. The second book was prefaced by Lucien Abenhaïm, then Director General at the French Department of Health.

Debates and drifts

Dr Kovess is by no means lacking in candour. Back in 1996 she was expressing concern about the difficulty of defining mental health. Five years later, she was noting: "The notion of mental health is a critical one; we must therefore clarify it to make it operational." Alas, this clarification was confined to the WHO definition. Quite conscious of the problem, the author concluded: "Exact knowledge of the processes at play in mental health has not been thoroughly established, and to a certain extent leaves room for debate." It is not sure whether we are going to be able to rejoice at the prospect of a debate that would end up admitting the inconstancy of the discipline. It seems more likely that the same procedures of statistical calculation and expert consensus will be imposed so as to seal once again the respective importance of the *biological, psychological*, and *social* factors that define the said mental norm.

Unlike Canada (one of the pioneers in the discipline), France has not adopted the WHO definition. This is why the author adds the following detail:

> In France there does not exist, to the best of our knowledge, any official definition of mental health. There is, however, a circular from the Ministry for Health that describes the main objectives and orientations of policy making [...] in mental health. (Kovess, 2001, p. 9)

This worthy avowal indicates two immediate consequences: the definition of mental health comes from a ministerial power, and "mental normality" is national (not international).

If it is true that today's psychiatry cannot claim to be the only medical science that is not universal, it is because it is founded on a communitarianism that does not hesitate to stigmatise "populational categories" and nations. The consequences of importing the infection model into the domain of mental health have not failed to raise a few doubts.

The return of the dangerous classes

No sooner had it been drawn out of its limbo by a few original minds than psychiatry was beset by a chronic counting and classifying fever from which it still suffers today. Indeed, evaluation and its related practices still aim at ascertaining what really needs to be qualified in Jean-Claude Milner's terms as "the return of the dangerous classes" (Milner, 2005a).

Order

It is not easy to distinguish between public order disturbances and mental disturbances when one is poorly acquainted with epidemiology. For these scholars, "risk populations" are defined by the criterion of social disturbance. This is why the questionnaires that assess them target above all else the poor, immigrants, minimum-wage earners, the homeless, and ethnic minorities whose calendar and festive rituals differ from those of the autochthons and put their backs up. In the end, what are these manufactured classes if not a judgement about the mode of jouissance of an "other" that is hastily perceived as strange and menacing to the fragile equilibrium of social health? In the age of globalisation, slogans such as "Enjoy Coca-Cola", "I think therefore IBM", "10,000 songs in your pocket", and so on, affirm how just a small range of knickknacks and gadgets have come to assure the well-being of us all: the same jouissance for everyone. Singular jouissance, meanwhile, has become intolerable.

The environment is also being incriminated in the occurrence of mental disorder (NB: the common sentiment that "genetics will prove it soon enough"). These fine notions, also baptised "bio-social criteria", are taken all the more seriously for having manufactured deviant populations in cunning studies on "categories". Two such studies on divorcees and the poor are not lacking in piquancy. It has been "scientifically" accepted that the divorced, the separated, the poor, and immigrants have poorer mental health than the rest of us. The poor are supposed to be the most fragile because they emigrate more frequently and unfortunately have the bad habit of marrying their own kind. Epidemiology has yet to establish "mixed" studies on divorced, immigrant, and poor individuals who have re-married with other poor individuals from whom they have separated once again. More extensive means and more time would surely rectify this shortcoming. Given the rapid spread of solitude and pauperisation across the face of the planet, the evaluated world shall soon be no better off than the world of Dr Strangelove. The evaluation time bomb has been spreading its harmful effects without the slightest analysis of the discontent it forces upon our civilisation. Without a clinical study of civilisation, there is little chance of a clinic of the subject coming into existence.

It would be unfair not to mention the fine study devoted to mental unbalance in the wealthy. Rest assured, the exceptional status of this evaluation of the rich confirms the general rule that poverty is a primary risk factor for "mental disorders". Although this evaluation is, needless to say, an oddity, we should specify that this is down to the country in which the study was carried out: Sweden. For the expert evaluators in epistemology, there does not seem to be any doubt that these results are due to the disappearance of paupers from this fine country. What if others were to get wind of this?

Disorders

The stable mental health of women is a legitimate preoccupation in nations keen to ensure their longevity while respecting their age-old traditions. The colourful populations of these nations, which make for their richness, would therefore be well-advised to follow the recommendations issued by the epidemiologists. For example, the absence of any intimate relationship with a male partner or the presence of more than three children in the household are "scientifically validated" criteria for a risk of "depression". Any nuances in sexual preference or in bereavement, and the nuance between melancholia and sadness, which resist the questionnaires and their calculations as we have seen, but which can pave the way to a truth that remains in abeyance, do not seem to have caught the attention of the academic psychiatrists who were busy falling in line with a Malthusianism they deemed to be fully deserving of a few sacrifices.

We may recall that the practice of questionnaires, sometimes with slight variations, does not always provide the "individual" with the right box for him to tick. This is particularly the case when it comes to the detection of psychoses. Since the diagnosis of paranoia first disappeared from classificatory systems like the DSM, "schizophrenia" has come to name practically all the psychoses. Thus, the risk that is being incurred is no longer that of the dangerousness of *chagrin* with its consequences of *passages à l'acte* (as clinical practice had been teaching for the last two centuries, and which the ever more numerous school shootings keep confirming). No. The only problem feared by the supporters of CBT is that of consistently bad statistical results that may well send schizophrenic subjects packing, thus threatening the reliability of the evaluative enterprise. Furthermore, the questionnaires are not addressed to "individuals" suspected of criminal acts, individuals who nevertheless stand in need of rapid diagnosis. The suspicious practice of the questionnaire then takes on strange tones, bearing a close resemblance to certain forms of denouncement, but without this prompting any special measures. Nor are the "sensitive" questionnaires on "violent behaviour" towards women and children or questionnaires on "addictive behaviour" destined for the parties concerned. To reach the highest degree of objectivity, the assessor's questions are put to neighbours and clients in the local café, "because that's where everything gets spoken about and everything is out in the open" (Kovess, 1996, p. 83). There you have it for the thrust of the pro-CBT science of evaluation that is driving out the psychoanalytic clinic on the grounds that the latter is not sufficiently scientific.

Mental disability

In the nineteenth century, psychiatry held that poverty was conducive to madness. We might be thankful that this assertion, which clearly sullies the honour of the discipline, became a dated and forgotten rarity, but this would be to fail to acknowledge the forceful spread of evaluation which, shrewdly backed by epidemiology, has brought the model into widespread use for underprivileged populations in their entirety.

Indeed, epidemiology does not recoil from asserting the organic cause of "mental disorders". The term "handicap" (which was judged too compromising) has now been replaced with the term "disability" (which is supposed to be more politically correct) without any change in the meaning. Updating the lexicon contributes advantageously to the evolution of mentalities, and so "mental illnesses" are being transformed into a host of disabilities that bear the same name. The reasons for this are both economic and moral. It did not take long for them to realise that it would be less costly to pension off a subject because of a disability than to include him in the healthcare remit. Epidemiology has thus been efficiently contributing to the foreclosure of the subject. This can be seen in the form of an exclusion that is very concerning, particularly in Canada. When the *Evaluator* Forum was held in Paris in 2004, Dr Patrick Pelloux, a renowned A&E specialist, spoke about the disastrous consequences that this evaluative policy has had in Montreal. The "mentally ill", renamed "mentally disabled", used to receive benefits before being divested of them when budgetary cuts were introduced. Then they joined the down and outs on the city streets, of which there were more and more.

However, using "disability" instead of "disorder" is no longer a choice dictated by economic factors alone. It also falls in line with the sanitary prejudices of the evaluators. The evaluation questionnaires no longer being sufficiently accurate, other "more reliable" questionnaires are invented, which, being riddled with the same ills, are replaced with others still. Not one sector in university psychiatry is safe from this evil. Some of them, however, have started to wonder whether an exponential need to count might have been finding some satisfaction in the epidemiologists, and whether they in turn have been subject to a categorical imperative of their own making that runs: "evaluate, plan, rehabilitate".

Rehabilitation (which is a term borrowed from the magistrates) presupposes a prior condemnation, but epidemiology is playing judge and jury, infringing upon the right of defence. With the exception of the study mentioned above, its questionnaires never address the more affluent parts of the population. Furthermore, were they to do so, what has been seen as mental dysfunction in the poor would most likely be judged mere whimsy in the rich, depending on their standard of living. Doesn't the moral of the story run as follows: *depending on whether you are mighty or miserable, the judgements of the evaluators will find you guilty or not guilty*? The will to know everything (which is the underlying principle of evaluative psychiatry) gives some idea of the Kafkaesque use to which these kinds of study could be put. Here, the American exception seems to be quite enviable. The most fanciful ideas will not easily lead the state to interfere in the private life of its citizens and decide what is good for their "mentality" on their behalf. The epidemiologists make an outward show of their socially rehabilitative altruism, but more secretly they are driven by a will to discipline and punish. What has changed since Foucault's time is that the emphasis is being laid more and more on prevention control. Nowadays, the goal is to discipline and banish.

The foreclosure of history

Biology is not particularly helpful when it comes to clarifying the logic behind epidemics of the mind, and so the epidemiology specialists came up with the idea of extending the examination of the mental ill to include their cultural particularities. These numerous and oh so erudite studies, which we are going to be looking at now, command great authority in the universities. We owe them to H. B. M. Murphy, professor at McGill University in Montreal. They date from the start of the twentieth century, but are quoted and revived in Dr Kovess's books. They examine the epidemics and mental illnesses that were once rife in Jewish and Irish communities. Why the Irish? The question is not so out of place. It has the value of putting us on the path of history, the same that is today being foreclosed by psychiatry.

The data Murphy drew on to establish his diagnoses of manic-depressive psychosis in Jews date from 1901; the data that conclude in schizophrenia in the Irish date from 1911.

In one of her books, Dr Kovess makes reference to both after the following introduction:

> Cultural affiliation was the object of epidemiological studies that were carefully reported by Murphy in his work on comparative psychiatry (Murphy, 1982; Murphy, 1977). In 1901, Fischer in New York and Plicz in Vienna remarked on the particular vulnerability of Jews to psychiatric problems. Even though alcoholism was very seldom found, hospitalisation rates ran high. In fact, this vulnerability was specifically linked to manic-depressive psychosis for which the hospitalisation rates in the Jewish community were twice those of other communities. This same fact can be found over and over, regardless of the context, whether in Frankfurt or Vienna, where care was readily available, or in Poland; whether in urban regions or in rural areas. In 1911, Pollock noted that immigrants of Irish origin had a psychiatric admission rate that ran four times higher than other immigrant groups. A few years later, the author used standardised data the better to compare the different cultural groups, and found that admission rates for schizophrenia among Irish émigrés were the highest in the United States. (Kovess, 1996, p. 45)

For a long time now, the practice of the consensus, judging mental illnesses to be just as shameful as alcoholism, has been caring less for the exactitude of the diagnosis than for putting itself at the exclusive service of the regularity of "scientific" facts that have to be forced into existence.

From simple calculations, they extract a culture/madness ratio, from which in turn a law will be devised, uniting them and making statistical reality pass over into factual reality. This was how Murphy calculated that Irish nationality and Jewish religion are causal factors favouring psychoses. Let's take a look at where the reality of these statistical facts leads us.

Irish schizophrenia

A quick perusal of the resources of my personal library (which reflects my interests and is weighted more towards the Jewish question than Ireland) only offered up an entry in the *Encyclopædia Universalis*. This did little to remedy my ignorance of Irish history, but it was enough to confirm that the dates that Murphy retains do in fact correspond to crucial moments in that history. The political crisis of 1840 led to a severe suppression of mass demonstrations against the Protestant-defended Union. Exacerbated by the 1846 famine, then further aggravated by a cholera epidemic, the crises decimated millions of Irish men and women, equal to a quarter of the population, and triggered a massive wave of immigration of Irish Catholics to the United States.

History teaches us that persecutions leave indelible traces and frequently get the better of tortured subjects who, as often as not, will never come to terms with subjective experiences such as these. The honing of some torture methods can even generate experimental psychoses. The Real of the persecutions that the Irish endured deserves more than these few brief remarks, but it is highly likely that a considerable number of them never got over this. They remained marked by the Real of this war that has only recently come to an end. But should the Real of a war, albeit a "civil" one, be mixed up with the real of psychiatric pathologies?

Jewish madness

Shortly before the vote on the Accoyer Amendment, Georges Bensoussan's erudite work, *Une histoire intellectuelle et politique du sionisme, 1860–1940*, was published by Fayard (Bensoussan, 2002). The places and dates that Murphy cites can be found here in the right place: the contemporary history of the persecution of the Jewish people. The second chapter on "A state of dereliction" gives an idea of the fate of

Jews in Russia during the collapse that followed the 1881 assassination of Tsar Alexander II. The first pogrom against the Jews took place one month later and spread rapidly across the Pale of Settlement.

Going by the etymology, "pogrom" was already a version of the final solution to the Jewish problem in the sense that Jean-Claude Milner employs it in his book, *Les Penchants criminels de l'Europe démocratique* (Milner, 2003). In Russian, *po* means "totally" and *gromit* means "destroy". Therefore, "pogrom" means "the total destruction of the Jews" of the Russian Diaspora. This version of the final solution to the Jewish problem was still to rely on hand-to-hand combat. It knew neither the efficacy nor the industrial scale of the Final Solution.

The publication of accounts of these historical facts allows us to form a grasp of the consequences that the pogroms had on the Jews of Russia. I noted the following details amongst others:

> There were waves of collective terror; the men remained petrified; fear had worked its way into the very foundations of Jewish existence in the Russian Diaspora; the children were frightfully pale and thin, wrinkled as if they had grown old ahead of their time. (Bensoussan, 2002, pp. 43–92)

It is hard to read these testimonies without thinking of those of Primo Levi describing the *Muselmann* in the Nazi concentration camps. The Real of this subjective experience turned them into living dead, feared by those who had not given up on survival. Bensoussan was surely thinking of this when he wrote:

> Despite the high number of pogroms and the length of the riots, the number of killings was limited. Doubtless because we tend to reason by measuring things against Auschwitz, we struggle to comprehend the horror of this situation in the eyes of its contemporaries. We find it hard to understand why these massacres formed such a cut-off point in the Jewish world of that time [...] and in the world at large; think of the indignant reactions in the West, Victor Hugo for instance, who seized the occasion in one of his final political engagements. The trauma was all the more violent given the confirmed complicity of the local authorities [...], the police, and [...] the justice system. (Ibid., pp. 44–45)

These persecutions, which saw the legalisation of anti-Semitism, gave rise to waves of emigration to Europe and the United States, up until the Jewish quota of the twenties. This emigration stretched over two generations and three continents. Indeed, the places that H. B. M. Murphy singles out were major destinations for persecuted Jews. Bensoussan mentions that between 1900 and 1925, a quarter of Russian Jews left the continent on which they were born, a shade under three million people. And he adds the following detail: "This was a permanent emigration, akin to that of the Irish" (ibid., p. 52).[3]

H as in "history", H as in "hatchet"

Biopsychosocial psychiatry has made Murphy's theses on Jewish and Irish madness its own (Lalonde, Aubut, & Grunberg, 1999, p. 1758). Widlöcher's *Traité de psychopathologie*, which is an authoritative book in the university, revives them too ("Psychopathologie des migrants" in Widlöcher, 1994, p. 830). Historical fact demonstrates just what a misuse of epidemiology "statistical fact" entails: it does not come down on the side of history, but on the side of foreclosure, thus opening the door to revisionist theses. The facts have been number-crunched, and man reduced to a few statistical figures—which are occasionally tattooed on his skin. In the 10th January 2004 edition of the French newspaper *Le Monde*, Giorgio Agamben criticised the use that could be made of this by the police (Agamben, 2004), and the very same day, Philippe Sollers expressed his concern in a brilliant speech at one of the Forums (Sollers, 2004).

Who would even dream of contesting the transmission of nationality from parents to children? But doesn't this beg the question as to whether this transmission is due to the laws of Mendelian inheritance or Parliamentary laws. If national belonging is consistent with the regularity of a scientific law that accounts for the causes of mental illnesses, then epidemiology could entertain a simple change of nationality as an effective preventive measure. Perhaps, in this way, naturalised Irish would no longer be liable to be judged schizophrenic. Similarly, it is not false to say that one is Jewish from one generation to the next, but wouldn't an eradication of Jewish difficulties be accommodated by religious conversion? Once converted to other religions, they would doubtless cease to be diagnosed mentally ill. If it is true that the word infidel is used only for those who have the misfortune to belong to powerless minorities, then we can expect our academic evaluators to be devising other mental disorders, following the sway of power across the face of the globe, to separate the Mohammedan from the Christian too, not to mention the Croat, the Chechen, and the Tutsi.

Evaluative logic serves the domination of academic bureaucracy. By demanding to master human jouissance, it means to force the human being back to his native state as the offspring of discourse, that is to say, a product, a leftover: the object *a*. With regard to the Jewish people, François Regnault has admirably demonstrated this in *Notre objet a* (Regnault, 2003). Its status as a residue, as a waste product of human creation, is clearly revealed here. The Jew, the Irishman, and many others besides (Lévy, 1994), can occupy this place of object *a* for the Other in general and for the Other of statistics in particular. Like any tyrant, this obscene and ferocious Moloch only derives its power from the voluntary servitude of those who consent to it, from experts in consensus to the most basic citizen. Working in Jewish hospitals, as Murphy did, the better to study these statistical "facts", does not make them exist. As for citing respect for cultural differences as a pretext for collecting sociological data, this is merely an assertion that is flatly contradicted by its application to epidemiology in mental health. The ideology it harbours in the name of calculus does not strike one as being particularly well measured. Rather it confirms the limitlessness of psychiatric power, already condemned by Foucault (2006). Taking the hatchet to history surely requires greater prudence.

Flaw and failure

Epidemiology does not always lack critical spirit. It heeds two sorts of reproach: those it addresses to itself, and those that are addressed to it from without. The implicit avowal of the fiasco of the discipline haunts its self-reproaches. The assessors should be doctors, but such is not always the case. Whether or not they are doctors, however, results are being falsified. The assessments by non-doctors are not sufficiently reliable because they have been putting causes of mental disorder in the medical category when clearly they do not belong there. As for the doctors, they corrupt results when they get their patients to tick boxes because they cannot refrain from reassuring anguished patients. We are not calling into question the doctor's sliver of humanity but rather the impossible objectivity of evaluations. Epidemiology itself deplores the problems posed by these evaluations, which are never sufficiently accurate, which are becoming longer and longer, and which only ever mention disorders without being able to define mental health as a positive fact by which to establish these disorders. The author of one enquiry reported by Kovess was already lamenting this back in 1961. Half a century later, the problem is still with us. "Mental health" does not exist now any more than it did back then.

As for the reproaches addressed to epidemiology from outside the discipline, they may be summarised as follows: "it is expensive and it is pointless". In one of the books by the said epidemiologist, she does in fact note the absence of any concrete consequence of such inquiries. You may have quite legitimate cause for concern as to the cost to the taxpayer of these protocols in mental health evaluation, but you may also be wondering how long it will take before this centralised numerical data starts to be used coercively on a grand scale.

Prevention control encrypted by mental health epidemiology is going to be the deciding factor in the budgets that the state will allocate. Therefore, it seems quite certain to last until this false science and its harmful consequences appear in the clear light of day. Until then, how many epidemics of alien sightings or of complaints lodged against parents wrongfully accused of incest will we see surging up, as they have in France and the US? How many "unmotivated" attacks on high-profile public figures will there be, like the 2002 stabbing of Paris mayor Bertrand Delanoë, the assassination attempt on then President Jacques Chirac that same year, or the 2003 murder of Swedish minister Anna Lindh? How many murders of other figures in administration and local authority, like the Nanterre officials and councillors slaughtered in 2002? How many more suicides among the youth and the aged, the free and the incarcerated? Yet, Lacan's teaching shows that murderous or suicidal *passages à l'acte* depend on one and the same logic: the logic of jouissance. Once the clinic of the case and the clinic of the act have been connected, we are no longer at a loss.

Medical staff can be called to account for the transmission of catastrophic epidemics, and this is as true for the puerperal fever of yore and today's nosocomial infections as it is for the evaluative fever that will soon be spreading far beyond the confines of the "mental healthcare" failure currently affecting the US.

CHAPTER SIX

Bioreligion

> The more authority you have among men, the less it is permitted that I silence myself when you mean to compromise psychoanalytic discourse and enchain those who serve it.
>
> —J.-A. Miller, *"Letter to Bernard Accoyer and to enlightened opinion"*

The crisis of concepts

Classify and count

Dr Jacques Bertillon, who had a marked taste for order and statistics, one day struck upon the idea of classifying causes of death. Although he did omit "mental disorders", his nomenclature[1] was quickly adopted by the International Institute for Statistics where it acquired great notoriety, inspiring the WHO in their *International Classification of Diseases* (ICD), the rival to the North-American classification system that went on to become the *Diagnostic and Statistical Manual* (DSM). As soon as Bertillon's inconvenient oversight had been set right in 1938, the first nomenclature appeared with five psychiatric diagnoses: general paralysis (caused by syphilis); mental retardation; schizophrenia;

manic-depressive psychosis; and other "mental disorders". As we have seen, today we can count some three hundred diagnoses in the DSM and a hundred or so in the ICD. Let's take a look at what was in the making of this feat.

In the post-war period, a handful of psychiatrists from the Old World and the New engaged in a struggle to recycle the applications of classification and statistics that had been much maligned following the defeat of the fascistic ideologies. By 1948, at the time of the creation of the WHO, the ICD (already in its sixth version) was starting to take over. But in 1952, the American Psychiatric Association (which included many psychoanalysts) answered back with its first *Diagnostic and Statistical Manual of Mental Disorders* (DSM-I). The ICD-8, published in 1965, was followed by the DSM-II in 1968. Four years later, the APA went on the offensive again, deciding to eradicate psychoanalysis from the DSM-III. Begun at that time, it was published in 1980 and then revised in 1987. The 1993 ICD-10 was joined, three years later, by the DSM-IV, soon followed by its revised version DSM-IV-R. This was how, from one publication to the next, the architects of the international classifications, neglecting the difference between the living and the dead, increased the number of pages and diagnostics in their infernal creations to the advantage of the American DSM, which eventually gained the upper hand.

To carry off this exploit, it took the tenacity of a few psychiatrists who relished the advantages of calculated order and were determined to make the discipline triumph "scientifically". Worried about seeing psychiatry reduced to its lesser part under the combined effect of the capitulation of the British psychiatrists and the success of the youthful neurology (whose dazzling progress was allowing it to snap up the infectious encephalitides on which psychiatrists had been pinning their hopes, along with tumour-associated and neurodegenerative dementia and congenital pathologies) the psychiatrists worked relentlessly to modernise their practise.

Excluding psychoanalysis

Once the arrival of antibiotics had drained away a large portion of the "hereditary deliria" that hitherto had seen psychoses and bacteria lumped together, the psychiatrists deemed it more urgent to reach a common accord on the manufacture of "mental disorder" than to lose time observing the phenomena that so stubbornly eluded their gaze, blinded as they were by certainty.

Until the time that psychoanalysis was banished from the DSM in the mid-1960s, the specialists clashed with such doggedness that the discipline was under considerable threat. When finally they grew tired of the quarrels, which they judged to be linked more to "political" considerations than "scientific" ones, the academics in the WHO (who were won over to evaluation) set up a research group on "mental health", advising it to seek international consensus in an attempt to save it. This consensus was found once it became a matter of classifying the "mental disorders" that the psychiatrists had manufactured with such zeal and devotion. Thanks to the shrewdest in their ranks, the idea soon gained sway that every single one of us, alive and kicking as we are, is ill without knowing it. Therefore, each of us should be protected from the perils we may incur. This gave rise to the triumphant consensus of "mental health" which they managed to get the WHO to adopt, and which was accomplished with all the more pugnacity given that their survival depended on it, as did the survival of the biopsychosocial psychiatry they had just contrived.

To bring their enterprise to fruition, however, the university evaluators first had to ensure their supremacy over the practitioners who rejected this "modernisation" in the name of psychoanalysis. The DSM-III had succeeded in excluding any reference to the Freudian discipline, and it was also steering the vast majority of practitioners. This was why the academics set about ridding themselves once and for all of the former while indenturing the latter by publishing psychiatry manuals that would find a way to have them fall in line with this shift in theoretical reference, not to mention the shift in practice. It took nothing less than a "crisis of concepts", holding out the prospect of a scientific foundation for psychiatry in the stead of an ideology (psychoanalysis), to impose with all the fanaticism of theory the revival of practices that really ought to be qualified as a bioreligion.

Biopsychosocial psychiatry

This was how biopsychosocial psychiatry, in preparing the ground for the recycling of the old-fashioned ideas of the hygienists that flowered during the Second World War, would first come to prosper in North-American universities over the last two decades of the twentieth century, before next sweeping over Europe. The book that opened the way to prosperity came to us in France from French-speaking Canada: *La psychiatrie clinique, une approche biopsychosociale*. The first edition in 1980 numbered thirty-odd chapters, but in order to adapt to the hyperbolic rise in manufactured disorders that were being churned out statistically, endlessly multiplying and complicating the classifications, the last edition in 1999 was just short of one hundred chapters, spread over two thousand pages. The conquest of old Europe, which had remained impermeable to this brand of progress for so long, was still only a projection, however. We would have to wait until 1994 for Widlöcher (we have said quite enough about who he is) to notice the substantial interest that occupying this terrain might represent, provided it be enriched by a hint of national positivism: in particular that of Auguste Comte which is so amenable to calculus.

Thus, the thousand or so pages of his *Traité de psychopathologie* made up for Europe's delay, and he was backed in this enterprise by a clique of supporters of CBT in the universities who had converted to Widlöchian psychoanalysis. Numerous contributors to the book, partisans of the psychiatrisation of society, would become major players in the assassination attempt on psychoanalysis perpetrated in 2003.

"Scientific" fanaticism

Si vis pacem, para bellum

As we know, psychoanalysis is incompatible with the suppression of democratic rights and since its inception it has been hounded and condemned by totalitarian systems of thought and power. Academic biopsychosocial psychiatry has more than one weapon at its disposal to wage war against psychoanalysis: from the bastardisation of technological scientific progress, which has been hijacked to its advantage, to the boosted use of statistics in mental health epidemiology, anything goes. This is how the Canadian academics mentioned above came to assert that:

> [...] today, new cerebral imaging techniques are allowing us to see with ever-greater precision the functioning of a brain that feels and thinks, but also hallucinates and becomes delusional. Furthermore, the recent progress in the domain of the epidemiology of mental

disorders is shedding more and more light on the psychosocial factors associated with mental disorders, from a scientific basis rather than an ideological one. (Lalonde, Aubut, & Grunberg, 1999, p. 4)[2]

To remedy this untoward state of affairs, a dual Cross and Sword strategy was advocated, leaving psychoanalysis with the alternative: either face scientific "discredit" or submit to forced conversion to CBT. In both cases its disappearance would be inevitable.

The history of the sciences should, however, have been enough to warn the psychoanalysts of the APA of the peril of these alternatives that mimic well-set laws. Yet Widlöcher, attuned to the Zeitgeist, fell in step with them and transposed to France what the North Americans were deploring on their continent: the "paling renown" of psychoanalysis now that homosexuality had been taken out of the DSM-III under pressure from gay and feminist lobbies, along with the lack of *assessable* results from psychoanalysis. He decided to turn this around with the forced cognitivisation of psychoanalysis. We have already examined how he went about this. As for psychiatry in the universities, it decided to pursue the crusade against the still unsubdued psychoanalysis in the hope of preparing the consensual humbuggery that was supposed to restore peace among the shrinks. It rejected the name and the ethics of psychoanalysis in favour of the biopsychosocial model of mental "disorder" (ibid., p. 5).

The psychological model

As the Canadian book tells it, this model has two noble goals: "to resist the deification of models" (to be understood as psychoanalytic models) and "to promote a scientific humanism". Then, it admits its submission to the constraints of the economic profitability of "mental health", because *socioeconomic pressures from third-party payers demand tangible results*. Skimping on the scientific requirement for treatments, this model ensures the commercialisation of "mental healthcare" with the support of private insurance firms. This same logic has already won out in France. Dr Philippe La Sagna and Dr Carole Dewambrechies showed this back in 2004 with their analyses of the reconfiguration of the French Social Security system (La Sagna & Dewambrechies, 2004).

The psychological paradigm is duty-bound to impose the hegemony of CBT on the grounds that "these theories lend themselves to scientific verification much better than do [Freudian] psychodynamic theories." The word "psychoanalysis", which never seems to be sufficiently blotted out, is here replaced by the less compromising term "psychodynamic". Inflicting such models on patients entails a certain dehumanisation that the academic evaluators quickly set about clearing up:

> Models do not dehumanise a relationship, only the people themselves can do that in their relation to each another. Dehumanisation occurs when the doctor [...] puts the model before the patient.
> (Lalonde, Aubut, & Grunberg, 1999, p. 6)

This new humanism means to be judged on its intentions. Wouldn't it be more correct to judge it on its consequences? Let's go back to the case of one of these evaluators: B. F. Skinner. An admirer of Pavlov, Thorndike, and Watson, he made no secret of his conversion to *The Religion Called Behaviourism* once a generous extrapolation from a caged pigeon had ostensibly proven that man could indeed be manipulated. In *Walden Two*, he has his alter ego say:

> I am stubborn. I've had only one idea in my life—a true *idée fixe*. [...] To put it as bluntly as possible—the idea of having my own way. "Control" expresses it, I think. The control of human behaviour. [...] a frenzied, selfish desire to dominate. (Skinner, 1948, p. 240)

Skinner logically concludes in 1971 with *Beyond Freedom and Dignity*: "We can't afford freedom". *Time* magazine splashed it in big letters across the cover of its 20th September issue of that year.

This psychological model means to wipe out psychoanalysis and stipulate devotion to CBT. But without the psychoanalytic experience, the perverse unconscious fantasy linked to the death drive remains unrecognised and fully active. The analytic experience does not fall under the heading of the useful, nor does it entertain any calculation as to its profitability. Indeed, without psychoanalysis, it is hard to envisage any kind of humanism in this day and age.

The social model

The social model that is steering our psychiatrists has been taken from an epidemiology that is being revisited by a new generation of sociologists who are stigmatising "populations" at "mental risk" according to social, economic, ethnic, and cultural criteria. We have already broached this point, so we shall just give two examples here (one concerning the family, the other, poverty) that shed light on the jumble of prejudices that prop up this model.

Biopsychosocial psychiatry establishes its prognosis for a psychosis based on its ideal of the family. It judges the evolution of a schizophrenia to be more favourable in Nigeria than in Denmark (Lalonde, Aubut, & Grunberg, 1999, p. 6). Since Shakespeare, we all supposed to be aware of what is "rotten" in the State of Denmark: the break-up of the family. So, calling upon Lévi-Strauss's *The Savage Mind* would have no effect on our modern psychiatrists for whom "the noble savage" is he who resists "the break-up of the nuclear family".

Very early on Lacan showed that for each subject the ideal of the family is the product of a delusional familism (Lacan, 1988). According to him, the conjugal family that has become the dominant form is a result of the evolution of our societies. Thus, it has a residual function, the function of the object *a*, and this is also what guarantees its future.

On the other hand, for these academics, the ideal family truly and verily exists. Not only that, they also judge poverty to be a "factor" in mental "deviance". Thus they state that a greater number of serious psychiatric disorders are recorded in underprivileged social sectors. The recommended form of prevention control highlights the importance of healthy life styles, adding that:

> [...] setting up [specialised] establishments in rural areas [...] was not related to any segregative aim on the part of the politicians [...] but to the "enlightened" opinions of the technicians of the time who were persuaded of the benefits of life in the countryside. The lack of means did not prevent agricultural colonies being set up. (Lalonde, Aubut, & Grunberg, 1999, p. 15)

At the end of the day, are these "healthy lifestyles" anything other than the lifestyles of the state-accredited evaluators themselves?

Don't the memoirs of the likes of Jean Genet (reading Genet always comes in handy for the edification of the incredulous) give a strong idea of the consequences of such worthy intentions? More generally, to treat *mental deviation*, they suggest changing the environment of the "deviants". You will recognise here the principle of moving towns into the country and vice-versa. In the case of resistance to programmes such as these, at what point is the necessity of changing the people themselves to rear its head?

I have already shown what this ideology aimed at singling out "dangerous classes" owes to political calculations. But Widlöcher's *Traité de psychopathologie* highlights the same data. In the field of this academic psychiatry the "cultural factor" extends its empire over the organism with great severity. They state that, "it is likewise important to understand that these reactions to different treatments vary according to the culture, and this holds true even at the biological level" (Lalonde, Aubut, & Grunberg, 1999, p. 6). This argument pertains to the following: if treatments for "mental disorders" manufactured by the university are inefficient, the failure is not to be imputed to the shortcomings of their model but to a claimed inequality at the level of the biological constants. Yet, the universal presence of constants is precisely what makes biology a science. This does not inhibit our scientistic thinkers who state that constants are geographically dependent variables! Any correlation with the wealth of the nation in question or with industrial pharmaceutical interests is merely fortuitous, of course. In "scientific" psychiatry, biological inequality is a new piece of data inscribed in genetic code. This odd thesis does away with the very idea of science and sheds light on a third model.

The biological model

This third model comes from a social Darwinism promoted in the name of the progress of neuroscience, genetics, and biology. For our evaluator/psychiatrists:

> Today, it is clear that mental pathologies, which previously were known as functional pathologies, involve an incontestable biological cause that is the necessary condition for the appearance of illness, whether schizophrenia, affective illnesses, or even what used to be called neuroses. Nevertheless, *as yet* there are no reliable and specific biomarkers capable of setting a sure orientation for diagnosis and treatment. (Lalonde, Aubut, & Grunberg, 1999)

The *Traité de psychopathologie*, then *Les logiques de la dépression* and many other books by Widlöcher, repeat the same arguments; arguments that still stand in wait of any scientific proof.

The biological model marks the return of a belief in the same hereditary causality for mental symptoms that was promoted by the nineteenth-century hygienists and discredited by Pasteur's discovery. Once Pasteur's microscope had lay ruin to the idea that tuberculosis was a hereditary disease, caught red-handed but standing on their dignity, the psychiatrists bounced back by occupying the neighbouring field of prejudices that employs the appellation: "predisposition to ..." (Widlöcher, 1995, p. 103). This field was to offer them a saving respite before science came along again to turf them out. However, it was by virtue of this "hereditary predisposition", inherited from their elders, that these psychiatrists came to manufacture the biological model in the universities, affirming the genetic origin of mental disorders by recycling hackneyed social-Darwinist theories (Lalonde, Aubut, & Grunberg, 1999, Tome II, Chapters 73 & 74).

Whatever its variations may be, this model preaches the inequality of races. It was already rife in North America and Europe for a century before being applied on a larger industrial scale. Social Darwinism changed its name many times over the course of the twentieth century, but it never changed its content. Only one of its consequences has disappeared for the moment: eugenics. These theories were passed off by Herbert Spencer, amongst others, and then in the post-war period by E. O. Wilson's sociobiology, and then as anthropobiology by one of its more recent descendents.

For Spencer, social order reflects the biological inequality of races. Only the genetically fittest know how to adapt to the societies in which they live. Applying *On The Origin of the Species* to social organisation served to justify racism, and in particular racial segregation in the US, but also the anti-Semitism that led to the Nazi extermination of Jews in Europe. In France, the psychiatrists who fought, as did Lacan's close friend Henri Ey, against the murder of asylum patients who were judged costly and unproductive were few and far between. After the war, racialist theses discredited this social Darwinism, but it soon found a new name with "sociobiology" and came to be hailed as an advance in human science.

To Edgar Osborn Wilson, an eminent zoologist from Harvard who published *Sociobiology: The New Synthesis* in 1975, we owe the idea of the selfish gene, championed as the great step forward in Darwinism. His simplistic principle stipulates that all human behaviour obeys the "fundamental law" of the spread of the individual's genes. Wilson upholds the idea of genetic racial inequality, but prudently drops eugenics in favour of a less compromising genetic altruism. Racial and cultural inequalities are alleged to explain the risk "factors" behind "dangerous populations" who nevertheless need to be rehabilitated given the notion that genes and surroundings interact. This racism with a facelift gave rise to violent controversies, in particular following the critiques by Stephen Jay Gould, himself a biologist and a colleague of Wilson's at Harvard (Gould, 1981). Sociobiology has been changing its name, but not its theses, and depending on the current it may be known as evolutionary psychology, anthropobiology,[3] and other monikers besides.

Squaring the circle

The grave shortcoming of this biological, psychological, and social "model" has not entirely escaped the notice of the academics. Indeed, they have struck on the idea of drawing up a vicious circle, dubbed "circular causality", as a means of giving themselves a semblance of scientific rigour. The argument of the first psychological model (CBT) is put forward, and then, when its failings show through, the second (social) model is invoked to mask it. The faults of the second are in turn shielded by the third (biological) model, which will be aided if need be by the first (CBT). This is how "cognition, emotion, biology, and behavioural studies" manufacture scientific *laws*, and this is the kind of training that is being imposed on psychologists at the university.

The same ideas serve as the guarantee for the following kind of fanaticism:

> The biopsychosocial model rejects any rigid dichotomy between organicist and psychogenetic approaches founded on Cartesian dualism. [...] The model based on circular causality leads to a finer perception of the complexity of human functioning [...]. Medication modifies biology; psychoanalysis[4] revives the emotions; behavioural therapy has an effect on behaviour; the cognitive approach corrects erroneous cognition. (Lalonde, Aubut, & Grunberg, 1999, p. 7)

The return to obscurantism

These knowledges used in the manufacture of biopsychosocial symptoms are easy to sell, but their efficacy is dubious and thus they have been tending to reinforce contemporary discontent.

The crystallisation of discontent

Philippe Sollers has shown how this discontent has been structured by what Heidegger called "The Question Concerning Technology". Sollers shed light on the logic behind this in his article for *Le Nouvel Âne* by indicating that the sovereignty of technology is enjoying a global destiny now that "the earth has thus become a 'physics' department and man the 'psychology' department that shall forever be its game." He adds that the problem is no longer one of knowing whether we are for or against technology, but one of "deciding whether, in relation to technology, we are standing up straight or staggering" (Sollers, 2003, pp. 2–3). The different forms of evaluation and the responses to the problems it poses vary from one side of the Atlantic to the other, but also from nation to nation in Europe.

In France

The Canadian academics ultimately came out on top in the country of the *Rights of Man*. Their strategy was set out back in 1999:

> Endless flocks of swallows have been heralding a spring that finally is really going to arrive thanks to the cooperation of the *Références médicales opposables* (RMO), the *Programme de Médicalisation des systèmes d'information* (PMSI), the first consensus and accreditation meetings (even though they have been worrying some), and long-awaited inter-professional reflection on inter-sectoriality, which includes: connections between the sanitary and medico-social fields, and between the public and freelance sectors. (Lalonde, Aubut, & Grunberg, 1999, p. 16)

As we have noted and reiterated, the main players in the "overhaul of practices" are all university academics resistant to psychoanalysis. They opted for "scientific" psychiatry, either in the wake of 1968 or at the start of the eighties, when it seemed less risky to cognitivise the Freudian discipline. They made themselves known through the positions they took in favour of the Accoyer amendment. This was particularly the case for certain influential members of the French Federation of Psychiatry. Having curried favour with the legislative powers, they sought to coerce them to rally behind their cause in the name of Widlöcher's *Traité de la psychopathologie* (which already topped the essential reading list for the exercise of psychotherapy). The RMO [Opposable Medical References] entail, for economic reasons, a standardisation of medicinal prescriptions and treatments, and this includes the mental field. Moreover, the PMSI [Programme for the Medicalisation of Information Systems] allows for these computer files to be purchased by private insurance firms. Medical secrecy has now become a contradiction in terms. In this regard, Dr Didier Cremniter has given an account of the slide in academic psychiatry (Cremniter & Bognar, 2005, p. 20), whilst Professor François Ansermet, who teaches at Lausanne University, has shown how the tyranny of stupidity seeks to regulate everything up to and including the pathologies themselves. More recently, Dr Jean-Daniel Matet stepped forward to condemn the dictatorship that is operative in the so-called consensuses (Matet, 2004, p. 8).

Just as worrying as consensus is the accreditation given by the ANAES [National Agency for Healthcare Accreditation and Evaluation] to those who define good practice. The second *Forum des psys*, in November 2003, was devoted to this, and the director of the ANAES was invited. The television journalist Jean-Pierre Elkabbach agreed to chair the debate, which was transcribed in the second issue of *Le Nouvel Âne*. One can see how the ANAES proceeds: it does not shrink from using arguments borrowed from managerial ideology with an eye to imposing limitless administrative regulation whilst itself eluding any control. A few months after the Forum, the ANAES changed its name to become the HAS [Haute autorité de santé]. Catherine Lazarus-Matet described it humorously as already "Has Been" (Lazarus-Matet, 2005, p. 17). Nathalie Georges-Lambrichs has given a detailed description of its use of evaluation (Georges-Lambrichs, 2005, p. 16).

The bridge between the public and private sectors that the Cléry-Melin roadmap prepared was designed to serve the new "Mental Healthcare Policy". Dr Bialek and Dr Sidon, who first exposed the relationship between the Cléry-Melin roadmap and the Accoyer Amendment, showed how the underhand tactics of the ANAES stemmed from the same logic (Bialek & Sidon, 2004, pp. 4–5).

Finally, by gaining acceptance for their belief in "mental health", the academic evaluators ensured the extension of the power of psychiatrists, which would now be applied to all citizens, regardless of whether they were "ill" or not. This was how the psychiatrisation of society was slotted together. As guarantors of the social order inherent to the idea of "biopsychosocial disorder", the psychiatrists became *ipso facto* assistants of police administration. We know that Canguilhem was already voicing much the same concern in his time. This administrative function was gradually extended to all the main players in the medical, paramedical and social fields who were transformed into guarantors of public order. The will to govern, which is usually veiled in the university discourse, here steps out into the open.[5]

In Europe

A number of European countries were rocked by the situation in France. *Le Nouvel Âne* provided a sounding board for this emotion. Furthermore, in December 2003, Judith Lacan relayed a message of support from professors at Moscow State University who expressed concern at our predicament. At the time of their delicate exit from the USSR, the Russians themselves had refused a similar decision because a number of them had already learnt over many long years the hard lessons of a privation of rights (Judith Lacan, 2004, p. 25).

Antonio Di Ciaccia reminded us that in Italy the 1989 "Ossicini" Bill which regulates the psychotherapies may well have been inspired by Freud's "lay analysis", but the university-bestowed titles of "doctor" or "psychologist" are sufficient to conduct psychotherapies in the Italian state; it is not one's personal psychoanalysis that authorises one as a practitioner.

Dr Alexandre Stevens from Belgium showed how this necessary condition has been tending inexorably to become a sufficient condition not only in his own nation, but across a whole string of European countries. Canadian psychiatry has been working away at full steam to gain acceptance for its views across the length and breadth of Europe.

The Ten Commandments

The psychiatrisation of citizens is thus being brought to pass by converting psychiatrists to the dogma of biopsychosocial psychiatry. The Canadian manual, *La psychiatrie clinique, une approche biopsychosociale*, the veritable bible of this form of psychiatry, sets out the Ten Commandments to which psychiatrists must submit. They may be formulated thusly: consent to the loss of power previously conferred by the patient; submit to the power of the universities (biology, sociology, psychology); master (the patients) by means of biomedical technology and short-term therapies (CBT); make use of computer efficiency; measure psychical suffering and social adaptation; assess the biopsychosocial components of "mental illness" and "mental health"; train in the scientific methods of professional associations and institutions (their own); attend congresses organised by the pharmaceutical industry (their financial backers); promote this research (and reject psychoanalysis); and finally, popularise their science so as to fend against misinformation (i.e., to block objections from a public who are worried about such measures).

Bioreligion extols the virtues of the "rehabilitation" practised by CBT. The promotion of values such as these in a field that claims to be "scientific" is really quite astonishing. Nevertheless, once it has been admitted that mental symptoms are a genetic affair, nothing much more can be done. Only pity and charity can orient the psychiatrist's action. The Christian values of social mercy take precedence. As they stand, these values are not to be contested. What is to be contested is the fact that they do not declare themselves to be such, but rather pass themselves off as science. Professor Briole, former Clinical Director of Psychiatry at the military hospital Val-de-Grâce in Paris, has shown how psychiatry, since its break from psychoanalysis, has become disoriented and fallen easy prey to modern states obsessed with order (Briole, 2007).

Is it in the name of this same principle of benevolence that psychiatrists must submit to judicial procedures?—because psychiatrists now have to employ every legal means at their disposal to obtain the judge's ruling should they decide, in the name of this "science", that a citizen's refusal to "cure" his "mental illness" is unacceptable. As Claude Imbert highlighted in a remarkable editorial for the weekly news magazine *Le Point* on 16th January 2004, it is quite true that the delusional precaution that weighs heavy on the shoulders of our democracies carries with it the demand for a zero-risk society. The obligation to pick out the "dangerous classes" (Milner, 2005a, p. 42) turns the shrink into the first link in a chain whose task is to ensure social calm when Christian charity is no longer enough. "Mental health" will depend on the simple fact of conforming to the norms of society. Make no mistake about it: soon, anyone who says "no" is going to have to be re-educated. One question remains: how would our biopsychosocial psychiatrist have treated the man who said "no" on the evening of 18th June 1940, and whom the authorities back in his own country sentenced to death?

The redefinition of care and the increased *judicialisation* of the role of the psychiatrist are turning psychiatrists into managers of a newfangled healthcare system that must "satisfy the state's desire to lower costs in healthcare by transferring institutional budgets to community budgets". In France, the logic of the Cléry-Melin roadmap would guarantee the promotion of a managerial and administrative psychiatry. In the columns of *Le Nouvel Âne*, professor Hervé Castanet looked at the question of knowledge and asked whether the economic aspect of the affair might not belong to the logic of a "steering state" model whose design is at odds with medical prerogatives (Castanet, 2003, p. 8). Wasn't this already to be found in the Canadian manual when it recommended that psychiatry should adapt to the neurosciences and to neo-liberal economic policy with its correlate of pulling the plug on the welfare state? Within a perspective such as this, utilitarianism would reign supreme, unless the steering state were to prove to be merely a transition from the welfare state to a liberalism that is more respectful towards the values of democracy. From here on in, university training in medicine and psychology, like the other training methods, will have to adapt to the needs of commercial enterprises and their evaluation systems.

Forced choice

Today, it is common knowledge that *classifying, counting* and *excluding* stem from one self same logic that leads to the worst possible option. The only jouissance that exists is the jouissance of the living being, as Lacan noted with his formalisation of the "object *a*". Jouissance is hardly conducive to classification, since the latter fits much better to what is dead than what is alive. Classifying and counting share the same goal: the exclusion of the object *a* of the living being. Since this is impossible, the classifiers start by ignoring the difference between the living and the dead. Next, the opacity of the object *a* is denied and it ends up being extended to the being as a whole. It is no longer one part of a living being that has to be eradicated, but the entire living being, which is rejected in the interests of fabricating "unruly and dangerous" classes.

We can see very clearly what is compelling certain academics to usurp the signifier "psychotherapist". This signifier still basks in the aura of psychoanalysis, because for many people the mental field still evokes psychoanalytic practice. Therefore, for the time being, the term "psychotherapist" is not redolent of the horror of sanitary moralism. Yet, under cover of making this false science attractive by naming it "psychotherapy", we are in reality faced with a moralism that is walking off with our freedom. Lacan was already condemning this perverse aim when he wrote:

> This is the encounter in which the equivocation of the word "freedom" plays its part: thereupon, laying a plundering hand, the moralist always seems to us to be more impudent still than imprudent. (Lacan, 2006, p. 659 [translation modified])

CHAPTER SEVEN

The commodification of knowledges

As the previous chapters have shown, *The Failed Assassination of Psychoanalysis* was the result of the tightening grip of scientism in the universities. A close look at publications from a few academics over the last thirty years has given us an insight into its vices. Knowledge has, however, always been in the service of the Master of the *Civitas*, and when the master changes, the knowledge that serves him changes too. This is why the attacks on psychoanalysis have only been possible in the wake of the deep modification in the relationships between power and knowledge due to the combined effects of the capitalist discourse and the discourse of science.[1] Lacan tried to account for this articulation between knowledge and power with the formalisation of his discourses.[2] Today, we no longer know what the master might have been in Antiquity, but we can discern how the modern master is linked to the secularisation of the universities.

Discontent and symptomatology

Evaluation has spread like wildfire in those regions of the world that share at least two common features: they are democracies and they are dominated by capitalism and science. We may hypothesise that in these countries the evaluator's "knowledge" has seduced the master because it claims to stave off the decline in authority that has stricken them, along with the overflowing jouissance that follows from this.

This undermining of authority can be felt across all levels of society. From the head of the family to the Head of State, going via the doctor, the professor, the mayor, the priest, and so on, not one ministership remains unaffected. This decline is not a contingent phenomenon linked to what was happening in France in the late sixties, it is a wider expression of discontent in civilisation. Capitalism and science combined have accelerated authority's decline to the point that the signifying fabric has worn through, letting us see that the Other does not exist (Miller & Laurent, 2005). Now, to remedy this problem by creating a "high authority" (for health, for justice, for finance, etc.) reinforces the discontent it claims to treat. Far from reinstating authority (which is now impossible), it accentuates the mirage of authority by setting up evaluation as the new mode of *governance*.

This discourse of evaluation claims to be universal. As we shall see, it thereby favours the emergence of new symptoms that feed the sense of persecution and which can produce depressive states that sometimes lead as far as suicide. The number of victims has been rising in direct proportion with evaluation's penetration into places of obligatory socialisation, such as children's schools or the adult workplace. Initially in the automobile industry, then in major distribution channels, county councils, prisons, police forces, hospitals, and so on, anywhere in fact that the administrative organisation is conducive to the secularised power of bureaucracy, the *knowledge* of evaluation has continued to spark off one catastrophe after the next.

The commodification of knowledges

Today, the modern master is money, and it demands that knowledge be a market value like any other kind of merchandise.[3] We are seeing different forms of knowledge waging a merciless war as though winning portions of the market were enough to legitimise their pertinence without sparing a thought for the consequences. Globalisation is reinforcing the illusion that it is possible to produce a complete totality of knowledge that would be valid for one and all.

The financial unease that has been shaking the world since the end of 2008 corresponds in part to a logic of this order. One feature allows

THE COMMODIFICATION OF KNOWLEDGES 121

us to see this. In using a language that is reduced, as we have seen, to simple letters stripped of meaning (*a, b, c*, etc.), mathematics has dispensed with the question of knowing whether what is calculated actually exists. These little letters guarantee the universal vocation of science and make us forget that this language remains a discourse, in other words, a social bond between the mathematician and *each* of those concerned by science. The blinkering effect produced by the discourse of science has favoured the effacement of all the peculiarities of power: prior to the advent of science, the master was *embodied*; since the advent of science, he has tended to be *disembodied* because science tends to free itself from the living body and only targets matter that the signifier can catch hold of.[4]

The capitalist discourse too has a universal vocation that it derives from its use of signifiers reduced to numbers. Only once the monetary signifier has been reduced to a countable element that lies outside meaning does it acquire its universal dimension. Effacing the singularity of the signifier is also a formidable factor in the acceleration and spread of this discourse, because there is no master who can rein in the stampede and rival it on a global scale. This is why the *money-master* is transforming our planet into a gigantic enterprise for the extraction of surplus-value. Marx was the first to grasp its displacements—of subtraction and return—that crystallise class-consciousness with neither worker nor entrepreneur being able to make head or tail of it. Lacan paid homage to Marx as the inventor of the symptom because he was the first, before Freud, to have grasped what the economy of jouissance consists in with its perpetual back and forth. This is why Lacan's "object *a*, surplus jouissance" was constructed on Marx's model of surplus-value.

Over these last thirty years, capitalism has seized hold of the tools of science and has been profoundly modified by them. Correlatively, the regime of surplus-value has also changed. Financial (that is, mathematical) capitalism has relegated industrial capitalism to the ranks of an old-fashioned has-been. Capitalism is no longer limited to the extraction of surplus-value from a limited work force localised in a few factories in large industrialised nations. The planet itself has now become a giant "factory" where each earthling is considered to be a potential source of surplus-value to be extracted by means of mathematical equations. Yet, in this language of science, those who are concerned are not even aware of it. Furthermore, mathematical equations can be spread more efficiently from one side of the planet to the other once they have first swept aside the obstacle of the peculiar jouissance of the living being. In a second movement, however, the object *a* that has been rejected from these calculations makes its return by taking concrete shape. This is when the symptom becomes acutely crystallised in the form of a worldwide financial crisis.

Indeed, the efficacy of the discourse of "subprime lending" relies first and foremost on the trust bestowed in financiers, but once this trust has melted away, its claim to universality melts along with it. The illusion of a discourse that is valid for *one and all* comes undone and it appears for what it is: a social bond that only concerns humankind one by one. Indeed, there is no universe of discourse. Regardless of their number, each body is only affected by this discourse on a one-by-one basis. Profit and loss are formed from the same object: the high profits of the trader depend on the high number of consumers concerned by mathematical financial transactions, whether they know it or not. Only elaborate ploys allowed people to think they might treat profit and loss separately. The trader[5] is just as inseparable from the consumer as the worker is from the capitalist.

Evaluation forces itself on the modern master and seduces him by offering itself as a remedy to the necessary failure of the discourses of science and capitalism. It comes from the same universalising logic, however, and reinforces the dead ends of these discourses rather than setting them right. To form a more precise idea of this, it might be useful to wind back the clock to the first emergence of this evaluative discourse, whose devastating effects are now patent.

A new control

It is surely to be admitted that the discourse of evaluation stems from an interest in production and its control that was initially shared by a small handful of men. They were the ones who shortly before and then just after the Second World War made way for the establishment of the discourse of science in the industrial sector. In the US of the 1930s, Walter A. Shewhart (1939) along with three other American scientists[6] invented "process quality control" as a new method for the statistical control of industrial manufacture. They successfully applied this idea in Chicago's Western Electric Company where they worked. Quality control was not limited to the object produced. From the outset, it covered the full set of humans who were operational in production. "Quality control" is the name they gave to the widespread implementation of this control. At the same time, this same factory gained a certain notoriety thanks to Elton Mayo's studies on improving control of worker productivity.[7] The successful implantation of behaviourism that went along with this quickly transformed the plant into a laboratory and the worker into a guinea pig. For the first time, "human resources" were taken into account in a way that was justified from the outset by economic imperatives. Seen as calculable production variables, the worker and his qualities became the object of all manner of assessments that concerned in particular his happiness in the factory environment.

This humanised variant of *Modern Times*[8] is carried along by a will to apply the tools of science to a field that does not fall within its remit: behaviour. It seeks to force behaviour to be more rational in order to improve the worker, that is to say, the "producer", as well as the product itself. Precise calculation of the factory worker's happiness would no doubt provide the welcome impulse for the statistical control of the *entire* system of production. Indeed, the system of production has to be stabilised in order to limit the losses caused by the number of defective objects that have to be sorted and set apart from the consumable objects. At that time, however, the booming industrial economy in the US remained insensible to this brand of progress. They would have to wait for a deep economic crisis on another continent for the method to be exported and developed. The immediate post-war period furnished Japan with this opportunity, and they gave a triumphant welcome to Deming's Total Quality Control (TQC). In 1950, Kenichi Koyanagi, founder of JUSE (Union of Japanese Scientists and Engineers)[9] invited Deming to lecture on statistics as a management tool from end-to-end on the production line, from the receipt of raw materials through to the client's reception of the product.

The two men had more than one thing in common. When their respective countries had been at war, each had acted as scientific advisor for the improvement of productivity and quality in armament. Once the two countries were reconciled, they united their efforts to share their common taste for this new management practice[10] with the members of Keidanren.[11] Once taken on board and improved by numerous different Japanese technicians, the practice continued to spread across the full gamut of new control techniques that have since ensured the international renown of post-war industry in Japan.

The warm welcome that industrial capitalism extended to the scientistic shift brought about by this handful of scientists made evaluation emerge as a trustworthy "knowledge", and it gradually colonised other non-scientific knowledges by submitting them to its power.

Imposture

The machine of evaluation tries to efface the following fact: evaluation is always carried out by a subject, and so his judgements and his beliefs will invariably be subjective and cannot be eliminated from the assessment scales. What is evaluated cannot, however, mask the fact that evaluation always consists in substituting quantity for quality. Furthermore, crossing the frontier between quality and quantity, between the tangible and the measurable, is at odds with the discourse of science precisely because this quantity/quality substitution claims to reintegrate what modern science has necessarily rejected from its field of study since its inception. Scientistic thought carries on as though knowledge could be a full totality that would never come up against the limits of the impossible.

Modern science was established only when it gave up notating the tangible data of quality, thereby invalidating the physics that had held sway since Aristotle. Once it had left the world of quality behind, physical science moved into the world of mathematics. The discourse of science achieved this separation between quantity and quality by using letters that were stripped of any quality. Since the advent of science, these same laws have been operative on earth as in the heavens. What eludes these laws and stands in the way of any idea of absolute rationality is the quality of Being and the Real dimension of this Being. All that is quantifiable, which is physical data, resides within the discourse of science. Quality, which is an attribute of Being and the real, resides within metaphysics.

In other words, the advent of science ushered in a new mathematical physics, whilst the "Freud event"[12] that corresponds to this knocked metaphysics sideways. The discourse of psychoanalysis was constituted when the desire of one man made room for the opacity of the psychical symptom (as the quality of Being and its Real), which it is impossible to lodge in the discourse of science.

Evaluation claims, however, to colonise this impossibility entirely, by means of its *quality* questionnaires. The imposture consists in setting up a substitution of quantity in the stead of quality to make us forget that "quality control" always concerns the human being and his productions. Nevertheless, the most abject part of this enterprise lies in the way that it obtains your consent to allow yourself to be reduced to the state of an entity without qualities, one that can be encoded and measured like an object. So, regardless of the modality employed (whether one evaluates, gets evaluated, or evaluates oneself), the evaluator (even if he too is evaluated) has to squeeze out the subject's consent to be treated as an object. From this, the evaluator draws a perverse satisfaction.

From the man of quality to the man without qualities

As we have seen, the discourse of evaluation was born in the pre-war US from the eagerness to eliminate flaws rather than have faulty products that were too expensive to sort. The scientistic bent, preoccupied with rationalising production,[13] then came up against refusal from the factory owners because the hierarchical organisation of Taylorism still held strong. During the war, however, industrial production gained in quality, including those cases where the factory-tailored product was death. In all likelihood the Shoah turned the authority of the divine master pale in his powerlessness to put a stop to it. The monotheisms and their churches still bear its scars today. Among the many consequences we may note the following: the modification in the regime of jouissance that had until then had currency in our democracies. Science and capitalism, now allies in a mass production of death the likes of which had never been witnessed before, showed greater power than any divine God. Thus, ensuring the decline of His authority, they showed just how outdated Victorian puritanism had been by producing a new, less bashful, subject. So much so that Lacan qualified this subject as shameless (Lacan, 2007, p. 190). This brazen liberation from shame still typifies the *Westernised* world today.

Once it had been penetrated by the discourses of science and capitalism, Asia could no longer escape the decline in authority affecting the Western democracies. Until its capitulation, Japan had been endowed with a theocratic leader. This was a form of power that had long blocked the way to the penetration and development of science, and no doubt capitalism along with it since the latter adapts very poorly to a strong centralised power.[14] The absolute power of the master, the emperor (descended from God) or the Tsar (by divine right), is generally coupled with an efficient bureaucracy. This was why, once they had been secularised, these sorts of regime tended to favour the installation of bureaucracies. Taken in hand by a *saviour*, as was the case in China and Russia, they managed to delay the joint development of science and capitalism by half a century.

The situation in Japan was different.[15] The sovereign, descended from the Sun spirit, was the head of the priests. The power of the emperor was, however, for a long time relayed by military chiefs who upheld a deep-rooted gentlemanly tradition. The Shoguns, Japan's official regimes from 1192 to 1867 (the start of the Meiji Restoration), constituted a powerful military counterforce. Unlike the other "theocratic" regimes in Asia, Japan's powers could not draw on the knowledge of the religious castes, which were simply not powerful enough. After Hiroshima and Japan's surrender, however, the emperor was forced to abdicate his divine right. Disarmament and the pacifist Constitution of Japan (Seizelet & Serra, 2009) accelerated the decline of military tradition and the counterforce of its castes (Victoria, 2006). Penetration by the discourses of science and capitalism was thus facilitated by two elements: on one hand, imperial might was powerless in the face of these defeats, and on the other, the knowledge of the learned,[16] in particular the religious learned,[17] did not manage to organise itself into a counterforce.[18]

Once the country had been disarmed, the military tradition of the gentleman, the man of quality, was transposed into the organisation of the nation's political life and its companies. The scientistic bent of American scholars steeped in democratic ideals slipped easily into the functioning of the factories. Without doubt, this was where the alliance between American rationality and the Buddhist and Shinto religious traditions was struck. After the defeat, the magic of the religious systems, essentially those of Shinto, had been so undermined that it could no longer guarantee the protection of the "enchanted garden" that Japan had once been, now faced with American economic rationality and its scientism. Its religious traditions were conducive to the implantation of the discourse of evaluation[19] inasmuch as Buddhism's comparatively rational religious regulation of life[20] also organised life in the factories. It gave high priority to the group format and to solidarity, and it favoured widespread mutual-control processes. Thus, this control was exercised both in the service of the common good and in the service of evaluation. It conferred the role of bureaucrat upon each citizen while making him participate in the traditional Japanese ideal of the *man of quality*. Calling upon suggestions, in return for pay, imparted worth to each worker who delivered his know-how in evaluation questionnaires, which then provided the yardstick by which he was to be judged.

Evaluation was made all the more welcome in Japan given that this "enchanted garden" possessed neither a clergy nor a lettered class who were sufficiently well organised to curb the readiness to install Total Quality Control (TQC) and temper the zeal of those who fervently took it on board.

TQC thus defined a new industrial economic policy that was presented as a horizontal system. Participative and paid "democracy" rendered the verticality of Taylorism's paternalist and authoritarian model null and void. From one system to the next, the advent of the evaluator went unnoticed. It was much less perceptible because the evaluator's exercise of power implies that he conduct himself as a group coordinator who gains the trust of each worker. The knowledge that assists this policy is established on the basis of a continuous transformation of each piece of information into a calculation, including the decisions to be taken at each stage of production so as to be able to stake a claim to the dignity of *scientific knowledge*. This *knowledge* masks over the evaluator's power grab. Thereafter, the use of calculus effaces that much more the ideal of the man of quality, to the advantage of the calculations of the man without qualities.

Depending on the taste of each evaluator, TQC in production is more or less supplemented by the worship of performance.[21] For example, Shigeo Shingo,[22] obsessed as he was with machine failure, reduced repair times, whilst Taiichi Ohno,[23] who was interested in "lean manufacturing", perfected the Just-in-Time strategy. Once the product has been improved by scientific techniques, the only *quality* issue that remains to be solved is that of service (i.e., the control of the *human factor*). The cognitive-behaviourists took it upon themselves to improve evaluation in such a way that it would tend increasingly towards zero defects. From TQC to "quality circles" and *Kaizen*,[24] there is an open invitation to the permanent control of human quality. Tracking human defects is set up at the heart of evaluation from the very outset.

A new policy

The policy of evaluation therefore perfects preventive control procedures in order to improve productivity. The concept of quality has no doubt proved so seductive because at first it seems to restore an initial defect to its rightful place—the original fault of man who does not function like a machine—but which may be *totally* remedied thanks to "quality control". Indeed, quality is sold as a surplus-value that is to be captured at any cost as a means of enhancing the price of the product or service. The "quality label" certifies that human faults have been tracked down using all the available technical means. The "zero-defects" concept that lies at the heart of evaluation strategy targets the jouissance that invariably produces a symptom. Thus, the degree zero of jouissance that constitutes the evaluator's ideal (because it would allow everything to run smoothly) is the inanimate state. For the human being, this means death. The portion of jouissance that can be elaborated by entering the logic of discourse can manifest itself only in accordance with two signs: either a plus or a minus, but never zero.[25] Thus we understand that this discourse is merely a "male fabrication" that gets zero and minus one in a muddle.

Japan's economic miracle, which inundated the world with universal ready-to-enjoy gadgets, left enough of a mark in hearts and minds for its methods to go on to be widely exported. After the war, evaluation first went back over to the US and Canada, which then served as the world's arsenal. The warm welcome from democratically minded religious communities then reinforced its greater autonomy and scope, before it arrived in the European democracies. Evaluation does not limit itself simply to making shameless subjects fall in line. From the outset, it has privileged know-how to the detriment of knowledges that are judged sterile for production and unnecessarily dangerous for companies, because it imposes its "knowledge" and only this knowledge. And so, it goes on actively rejecting the republic of letters, and psychoanalysis along with it.

The discourse of evaluation thereby contributes to imposing management on nation states as though they were companies. This ideology prompted industry to pass from the era of sorting to the era of control and prevention, and then to the era of strategy. The watchwords of evaluation, its master-signifiers, have invaded everyday life. Thus, the Toyota way is tending to replace the American way of life that governs us, the better to serve the logic of the steering state. In this context, psychoanalysis is more indispensable than ever when it comes to attending to the symptoms and analysing the discontent produced by this discourse. Psychoanalysis addresses itself to subjects only on a one-by-one basis, and thus makes a place for the singularity of those who desire to orient themselves in relation to what constitutes the opacity of the symptom.

A FEW WORDS OF CONCLUSION

Let's make it quite clear that *Scilicet* is closed to no one, but anyone who has not featured in it will be hard pressed to find recognition as one of my pupils.

—J. Lacan "Introduction de *Scilicet*", 1967[1]

The Real that inhabits us provokes its own misrecognition, yet makes itself felt both in the opacity of the symptom (specific to each of us) and in the opacity of discontent in civilisation. Psychoanalysts have a duty to interpret this opacity. They rose to the occasion recently when children and teenagers found themselves being taken hostage by a scientistic discourse: in 2005, Inserm went so far as to stigmatise infants who stole Lego bricks by marking them out as future delinquents (Inserm collective, 2005a), and the HAS (Haute autorité de santé) gave a platform to experts so that a "scientific" link could be established between these hapless infants and problem teenagers, dubbed "psychopaths" for the occasion. A large movement of public opinion subsequently went up in arms, relayed by the press and media. It succeeded in taking the edge off of some of the more harmful consequences of this university discourse beholden to CBT (and which is still staking its claim to the "science" label). A more determined mobilisation should be able to put an end to it once and for all.

The survival of psychoanalysis depends on the determined desire of those who make themselves responsible for it. This book has afforded a few insights into the issues and consequences of the false forms of knowledge that were to inspire the bill on the psychotherapies. The new moralism that means to lay its hands on the freedom of the citizen through the forced psychiatrisation of our society is finding reinforcement, as we have shown, from a blinkered bureaucracy that is imposing the deceptive evaluation machine across all sectors of society.

It is hard to say whether the politicians of today, elected by universal approval, shall in time see how to detach themselves from the scientistic discourse that has been cultivated in secret by bureaucrats and academics, and whose consequences will not only be our nightmare, but the nightmare of the French Republic.[2] The prevailing discourse needs, therefore, to be analysed. When those who seek to govern become ever more numerous, there still remains, for each of us, the privilege of being a citizen, and, depending on one's desire, the possibility of being part of attentive and enlightened public opinion. In other words, it is still possible to say, today: "Thou mayest know".

APPENDIX I

The new Amendment

5th March 2009, 11:47pm, the National Assembly adopted the hereunder amendment at first reading. The amendment was proposed by the government, and modifies article 52 (known as the "Accoyer Bill") of the Health Act.

Mme Roselyne Bachelot defended the Amendment before the Assembly in person. M. Le Guen (Socialist Group) was very pleased that finally "something structural is being achieved with regard to the title of psychotherapist"; Mme Génisson chimed in with a similar remark. The commission's rapporteur also voiced his support for the text, which was adopted unanimously. Since the government has declared the Hospital Reform Act to be a matter of urgency, there shall only be one reading in each chamber. After the Senate's examination, the government will decide on the implementing decrees.

Amendment enabling the addition of clauses to two paragraphs of article 99 of the Code.

AFTER ARTICLE 22 No. 2083 Rect. NATIONAL ASSEMBLY 5 March 2009 HOSPITAL REFORM (No. 1210) Government Commission.

AMENDMENT No. 2083 Rect. presented by the Government ADDITIONAL ARTICLE AFTER ARTICLE 22, insert the following article: The third and fourth paragraphs of Article 52 of Act No. 2004–806 of 9 August 2004 on public healthcare policy are now to be replaced by four paragraphs as follows:

"A decree from the Council of State specifies the modalities of application of the present article and the conditions of theoretical and practical training in clinical psychopathology to be met by all professionals who wish to be included on the national register of psychotherapists. It defines the conditions under which the Ministry of Health and the Ministry responsible for Higher Education approve those establishments as are authorised to offer this training.

"Access to this training is limited to those qualified to doctorate level and having the right to practise medicine in France or to those qualified to Masters level in psychology or psychoanalysis.

"The Council of State decree defines the conditions under which those qualified as medical doctors, those authorised to use the title 'psychologist' in the conditions defined by article 44 of Act No. 85–772 of 25 July 1985 including various social order measures, and those psychoanalysts listed in the directories of Associations, are entitled to benefit from a total or partial dispensation for training in clinical psychopathology.

"The Council of State decree also specifies the transitory measures from which professionals may benefit if they have been practising psychotherapy for at least five years at the date of publication of the decree."

A brief summary

Given the sensitive nature of the troubles they seek to ease, which touch on the mental and relational intimacy of individuals who are often in a situation of great vulnerability, psychotherapists must be highly skilled and competent in order to tend to those who call upon them.

This is why it is indispensable for all those who use the title "psychotherapist" to have undergone theoretical and clinical training in clinical psychopathology during their studies. The concepts and approaches that will have been developed in this training require, so that they may be understood, a high level of study: Master II in psychology or psychoanalysis, or a medical doctorate.

Professionals who during their initial studies have already undergone all or part of the modules developed in this training will of course be able to benefit from total or partial dispensations. Quality training only exists when the establishment that offers it is a quality establishment, and this is why it is necessary to approve these establishments.

Moreover, it is necessary to foresee measures that allow the particular situation of professionals who have already been practising for several years to be taken into account.

APPENDIX II

"Scientifically" discrediting psychoanalysis and attacking civil liberties

The French news weekly, Marianne No. 369, 17th–23rd May 2004, published the following text which I am reproducing in its entirety. It deserves to feature in its original form, in spite of occasional repetition, for at least two reasons: firstly, in deciding to publish its violent indictment of psychoanalysis, Inserm was stepping outside its field of competence, and that was a first. Secondly, this blow, which sought to be fatal, would indeed have been so were it not for the large-scale mobilisation against the Accoyer Amendment which quickly allowed us to anticipate and soften its consequences. This was how the assassination attempt on psychoanalysis came to an end, once the publication of the Inserm volume had missed its target. Finally, we would like to indicate that in March 2004, Jacques-Alain Miller opened his Lacanian Orientation course (currently unpublished) to a series of critical readings of the Inserm volume.

What on earth is Inserm doing in this boat? By attaching its label to an expert report that claims to evaluate the psychotherapies, the Institute of Medical Research has strayed outside its domain of competence and is undermining a prestige that hitherto stood uncontested.

It is true that when Inserm agreed in 2001 to take on the mission entrusted it by the French Department of Health, which it subcontracted to a panel recruited from outside the establishment, the psychotherapy question was not yet a burning issue. It had become one, however, by the time the volume appeared: after the Accoyer Amendment on the regulation of psychotherapies, after its withdrawal in the wake of a campaign of public opinion that was headline news for several months, even though the legislative outcome was still in suspense, vigilance was extreme, as were the criticisms voiced in a lively language that conveyed the emotion being felt. Roland Gori, professor of psychotherapy, spoke of his "disgust"; Guy Briole, professor of psychiatry, condemned an "act of deception"; the report's authors themselves expressed their reservations as to the summary that was being presented, some even going so far as to dissociate themselves from it; practitioners were aghast and furious, and spoke out fervently, expressing their disagreement on the internet; the greater number of psychoanalysts, who are generally given to division, for once fell in as one in their condemnation of the report as a war machine against psychoanalysis; solid refutations were in preparation. In short, a hurly-burly! Nothing of the like had ever been seen in relation to Inserm.

In point of fact, it soon turned out that the report had a predetermined goal: to valorise the so-called "cognitive-behavioural therapies" to the detriment of all the rest, in particular psychoanalysis and its applications. To obtain this result, the method employed was one of robust simplicity: there would be not a single psychoanalyst among the chosen experts, all of whom were promoters of CBT! What did the administration at the Ministry of Health stand to get out of this? Well, in a word: the prospect of lower social security costs. CBT offers short-term, pre-formatted treatments with clear-cut targets, whereas treatments inspired by psychoanalysis are unpredictable. But it so happens that CBT is poorly thought of in France, with barely ten per cent of psychiatrists using it, whilst two thirds of them draw on psychoanalysis. So, it was a matter of using the Inserm label for a marketing operation designed to accredit methods that had not managed to win over the public on their own strength. All this was served up in pseudo-scientific rhetoric, with figures and graphs left, right and centre, based not on experience, but on a literature, most of which was from the US, the authors of which were themselves CBT practitioners.

A comparative evaluation presupposes that the rivalling elements are comparable, but this is hardly the case here. Psychoanalysis in particular has nothing whatsoever in common with the cognitive-behavioural therapies.

For psychoanalysis, the symptom is not a "disorder", it is a silenced truth that needs to be heard. The symptom also includes a paradoxical satisfaction that leads to suffering ("jouissance"). Treatment is a dialectical procedure, which brings to the surface the weight of jouissance that words carry. Words encircle the truth without the subject being aware of it. Grasping these two faces of the symptom—language and jouissance—allows the subject to read his story and to make it his again. Then he can let go of a part of this jouissance and become responsible for its remainder in a life that does not necessarily conform to common morality, but is no less lawful for it. The psychoanalyst, having been analysed himself, is one who has detached himself from this fantasmatic jouissance. Free of prejudice, he can then enable the patient to invent his own bespoke response, the one that fits him.

For CBT, a symptom does not harbour a peculiar truth: it is a "disorder", that is to say, a malfunction due to faulty conditioning and defined by criteria that are the same for any patient. Therefore, the treatment is also the same for all and sundry, and is set out in handbooks. What is a CBT therapist? It is an operator (who may be a nurse, an educator, a psychologist, or a psychiatrist) who has learnt the handbook by heart, who applies the standard procedure point by point, and who imposes the matching response.

The basis of the method is the conditioning/deconditioning procedure. All cognitive-behavioural therapies are inspired by the Pavlovian theory of old. Pavlov was an early-twentieth-century specialist in digestive glands. He found that by systematically ringing a bell each time food is presented to an animal, one will soon be able to make the animal salivate simply by ringing the bell. There you have it for the basic model. The idea was to extend this model to the human being, by submitting him to authoritarian learning processes. In its day, it was discredited outright, but since then it has seen a resurgence in the US. This was achieved by integrating elements from the branch of psychology known as "cognitive psychology" which came to prominence in the 1960s. Cognitive psychology takes computer information processing as its model of the brain's function. Thereafter, this was used as the principle of the new "therapies" whose underlying postulate is something along the lines of: Russian dog + American computer = man.

This practice of sheer force is supported by moralistic prejudices that can be devastating for the subject who is made to conform to them, regardless of his own specific values and the peculiarity of his desire. This is the case in "aversive" procedures that aim to cure the patient by methodically anguishing him. For example, a child with arachnophobia will be put in contact with spiders until the anxiety stops, in spite of his complaints. This gives one to think that the sadistic fantasies of therapists may be finding a means of expression, just as they did in John Watson's time with his experiments on an eleven-month-old baby, or in the more recent electric shocks used on mentally-disabled patients resistant to this kind of treatment.

More generally speaking, the mainspring to these therapies is *suggestion*: the therapist uses the authority that is invested in him, the knowledge that is supposed of him, to impose his views with insistence. Freud gave up on suggestion because he saw that its results were not lasting, that it did not make symptoms disappear but merely displaced them. That was how Freud discovered the unconscious and invented psychoanalysis. Its results, though less rapid, are more sizeable and more durable because they are made to measure by the subject himself.

The ethics of psychoanalysis has nothing to do with the brisk mental orthopaedics of CBT. Is it really legitimate to put them both in the same "psychotherapy" basket? No legal definition of psychotherapy exists. This is not mentioned in the report, which uses a homemade definition cooked up by CBT. As a matter of fact, the report does not evaluate three different forms of psychotherapy, since it only takes into account approaches that have already been "cognitivised". It is not true that psychoanalysis has been "evaluated": analytic treatments strictly speaking were considered "unevaluable", and so the report only looks at short-term "psychodynamic psychotherapies", many of which are unheard of in France, and the rest are very seldom practised. But they make sure to add the word "psychoanalytic" in brackets, because this is all about discrediting by association rather than evaluating.

As for psychoanalytic theory, it stands to be "cognitivised". J. Cottraux, a promoter of CBT, recently referred to the cognitivisation of psychoanalytic theories by North American psychoanalysts, and was pleased to see "the recent appearance of an identical tendency towards this sort of bridge in France". Daniel Widlöcher, a member of a CBT association, also happens to be the current president of the International Psycho-analytic Association. He was the only psychoanalyst to be consulted for the Inserm volume. His theses inspired J.-M. Thurin, the reporter on psychodynamic therapies in the volume. In actual fact, psychoanalysis is never present in this text: a simulacrum of psychoanalysis is presented, with the sole aim of concluding in its inefficacy.

The misuse of statistics in this report brings into existence an "average man", but this man is pure fiction. Lacan says as much in an article published in *Magazine Littéraire*:

> First off, let's get rid of this average Joe who does not exist. He is a statistical fiction. There are individuals, and that is all. When I hear people talking about the guy in the street, studies of public opinion, mass phenomena, and so on, I think of all the patients I've seen on the couch in forty years of listening. None of them in any measure resembled the others, none of them have the same phobias and anxieties, the same way of talking, the same fear of not understanding. Who is the average Joe: Me, You, my concierge, the president of the Republic?

The notion of mental normality is a statistical definition that makes the average the norm. Whatever does not conform to this should not be viewed as an abnormality to be treated by rehabilitation and medication with the aid of CBT.

We would never get to the end of the string of biases, misuses, and manifold paralogisms that strip this report of any scientificity.

- To be scientific, a therapeutic method has to be reproducible, say the authors; they note that this is impossible for psychoanalysis; so they put their trust in the Health authorities who are "aware of the problem".
- The *Diagnostic and Statistical Manual* (DSM) is very badly thought of in France, due to its confirmed lack of reliability and validity; it is criticised by the authors of the report, and yet their study leans entirely on this manual.
- Far from being objective, the measures that serve to evaluate the therapies stem in reality from questionnaires established by and for cognitive-behaviourists.
- The efficacy of CBT boils down to the way it carves up symptoms infinitesimally. Judge if you will the following: the case of a woman

suffering from intense anxieties, one of which is to open her mail. After a few sessions of CBT, she is managing to open her letters, and she is sent away, having been cured and "efficiently treated". Another case: a schizophrenic is considered to have been treated with success and is recorded as such in the statistics when the therapist has managed to force him to conceal his "shifty eyes". Is concealment of something that causes suffering really a successful treatment?

- The selection of the bibliography is flagrantly partisan: the studies contested by the scientists have been kept on board because they are hostile to psychoanalysis; the studies by Inserm researchers who condemn the chosen method are ousted; this is also the case for some CBT supporters who were forced to note that their methods are not as efficient as other therapies.

The "scientific" proof of effectiveness is equally grotesque. The experts do not see any difference between a psychotherapy and a drug. One can understand how a doctor or patient might be unaware of whether a tablet is real medication or an inactive powder (placebo) in the context of an experiment where the efficacy of a treatment is being tested, but how can there seriously be a placebo for psychotherapy? Are the shrink and his patient supposed to be unaware that they are speaking? The effectiveness of a psychoanalysis is due to a determined desire to undergo psychoanalysis: how is this to be respected when one proceeds by the random, authoritarian drawing of lots?

Since the treatment is standardised, the strict application of what is in the handbook can be monitored under video surveillance. This method, which is practised in the US, suppresses all liberty of the subject along with any possibility of the psychoanalyst's act. The standardisation of the treatment implies the widespread robotisation of both shrink and subject. Are they counting on the anguished distress of their patients, adults and children alike, to ensure compliance? Evaluation, which was designed by and for the car industry (Toyota's Total Quality Control), scorns the dignity of the speaking being. Genuine researchers at Inserm have shown that this kind of assessment is impossible in psychotherapy. The results cannot be generalised, nor can the starting hypotheses be verified. Dr Plantade, president of the French Society for Child and Adolescent Psychiatry, had already voiced serious misgivings about the results of the previous Inserm report. It, too, systematically privileges:

[...] neurobiological and cognitive models of explanation, without taking into account clinical and psychopathological works [...], which has led three child psychiatrists who were part of this project to withdraw. (Plantade, 2004)

Today, the authors of this volume are voicing the same concerns.

The conflicts of interest are far-reaching. The experts are not independent but act as both judge and jury. All those whose opinions have been solicited are closely linked to CBT. Inserm, too, is playing judge and jury, because it also finances CBT research.

What is truly at stake can be deduced as follows: discipline and banish. The current Director General of Health has been following "epidemiologists in mental healthcare" who lean on a social Darwinism that states, for example, that paranoiacs are "more frequent in underprivileged areas" (Cottraux & Blackburn, 2001, p. 13). More generally, from this angle, mental disorders are seen as a fact of life for the divorced, the separated, the poor, and migrants; mental pathologies are recognised depending on religious or national affiliation. We are seeing the return of the "dangerous classes" who are to be disciplined and banished.

Certain economic issues have also been indicated: obtaining reimbursement, not for the intervention, but for the time spent: sessions of CBT last between thirty minutes and three hours. Not far down the line, we will be seeing patients clocking in at the consulting room. Failing to take into account the reality of social security, this is about trying to extend the third-party payer scheme to CBT-trained psychologists, nurses, and GPs. What fate would they like to see in store for those who do not apply these compulsory standards?

The psychoanalysts, as heirs to Freud and Lacan, are not asking for a reimbursement system. For them, the issue is an ethical one. One of the goals of this operation is to oust the clinical psychologists and psychoanalysts from universities so as to make them the exclusive reserve of cognitive-behaviourists.

These are, therefore, political stakes. In the context of the vote on the Health Act in April 2004, the publication of this report is a tactical manoeuvre that is part and parcel of a publishing strategy that includes: The Report by the Academy of Medicine (July 2003), the Cléry-Melin/Kovess/Pascal Roadmap (September 2003), the Accoyer Amendment (October 2003), the Mattei Amendment (January 2004) and the Inserm Report (February 2004). It is designed to influence legislators in order to obtain the status of "psychotherapist" under the exclusive control of psychiatrists who would be "super-prefects of the soul" (Bernard-Henri Lévy). This Orwellian programme to lay siege to civil liberties is to be eased into place by "scientifically" discrediting psychoanalysis.

So, we are faced with a social choice. The recent circular issued by the Ministry of Education (December 2003) is setting up a compulsory mental health record for our children, to be put in place after the summer break. As soon as they step outside of the statistical average, they are to be reported and declared abnormal. Is CBT, this veritable orthopaedics for the mind, about to be imposed by law? That would constitute an unprecedented attack on civil liberties. The problem goes far beyond political divides. The question for us, now, today, is the following: is this really the future we desire?

NOTES

Chapter One

1. This Amendment is Amendment 336 of the Public Health Code passed unanimously by the National Assembly on 8th October 2003. For an English-language translation of the relevant extract from the *Journal officiel de la République française*, see Miller, 2005b.
2. Jacques-Alain Miller is the founder of the World Association of Psychoanalysis (WAP) of which he was the first president. He is also the editor of the *Seminar* of Jacques Lacan, a position he took at the latter's behest.
3. France's National Institute for Healthcare and Medical Research.
4. *cf.* Charrière-Bournazel, 2003. Maître Charrière-Bournazel was *Bâtonnier* of the Paris Order of Lawyers from 2008 to 2010 and since 2012 has been the president of the National Council of Barristers.
5. On the question of the legal loophole that the Amendment sought to close, see: Maleval 2003.
6. *Le Nouvel Âne* opened up its columns to these representatives. See in particular: Normand, 2004; Hacquard, 2004; Ginger, 2004; and Grauer, 2004.
7. On this subject, see: Leguil, 2004.

8. Each of his articles may be consulted in the contemporary issues of *Le Nouvel Âne*, in particular, Lévy, 2008, which was presented at the *Forum des psys*, 9th–10th February 2008.
9. An English-language translation can be consulted in: Miller, 2005b, pp. 55–57.
10. *cf.* Fédération française de psychiatrie, 2003. At the time of the French publication of this book, the FFP was directed by Christian Vasseur.
11. I was also present at this debate, on which I wrote a report: Aflalo, 2004a.
12. On this point in particular, see: Roudinesco, 2005.
13. [*Reconnaissance d'utilité publique* (RUP) is a procedure in French law by which the state acknowledges an association or foundation as being of public benefit. This affords it specific advantages and a particular legitimacy. (Tr.)]
14. Éric Laurent was the 2006–2010 President of the World Association of Psychoanalysis.
15. [Since the French publication of this book, events have taken a more favourable turn in the UK with the 16th February 2011 announcement that the government was effectively abandoning its project of the state regulation of psychotherapy and counselling. (Tr.)]
16. See also: Miller, 2006a.
17. Gracián, B., "The sixth crisis: The estate and condition of this age". In: Gracián, 1681.
18. [Madame Roselyne Bachelot held the post of Minister for Health until November 2010. (Tr.)]
19. On 5th March 2009, a new Amendment replaced the Accoyer Bill. See Appendix I in this book.
20. *cf.* "The unanimous declaration of the thirteen United States of America", adopted by the Continental Congress on 4th July 1776:

> We hold these truths to be self-evident, that all men are created equal, that they are endowed by their Creator with certain inalienable Rights, that among these are Life, Liberty, and the pursuit of Happiness. […] That whenever any Form of Government becomes destructive of these ends, it is the Right of the People to alter or abolish it, and to institute new government, laying its foundation on such principles and organising its powers in such form as to them shall seem most likely to effect their Safety and Happiness.

Chapter Two

1. [The French term *jouissance* is notoriously difficult, even impossible, to translate. In psychoanalytic terms it indicates an "enjoyment" that lies

beyond the pleasure principle, and which may thus make itself felt in the form of displeasure or suffering. (Tr.)]
2. See also, (Miller, L., 2005, p. 7).
3. *cf.* "Excommunication" in Lacan, 1993, pp. 1–13; and Lacan, 1990b.
4. We shall come to this point in "The hypothesis of the Freudian unconscious" below.

Chapter Three

1. In Freud, libido designates both desire and jouissance.
2. Meaning is an effect of the signifier, and enjoy-meant is an effect that lies beyond the signifier, supported by the letter.
3. These ideas crop up frequently in Widlöcher's books, for example in the chapter "Le modèle de l'angoisse" in Widlöcher, 1996, pp. 241–243.
4. In this book, the study of "psychical disturbance" is complemented by a study of socio-cultural background (Chapter Four) and biological underpinnings (Chapter Five). On the idea of a biological, psychological and social unconscious, *cf.* Widlöcher, 2003, p. 207.
5. Serotonin is a neurotransmitter that can be found in the brain. It is implicated in the regulation of functions such as thermoregulation, eating and sexual behaviours, sleep, pain, anxiety, motor control, etc.
6. Widlöcher sometimes sees countertransference as a daydreaming activity. *cf.* Preface to Guignard & Bokanowski, 2007, p. 16.
7. Widlöcher seems to conflate telepathy and co-thinking. Amongst other occurrences, see: Widlöcher, 2003, p. 260.
8. On this point, one may consult: Lacan, 1990b.
9. This slide from the *psychoanalytic* to the *psychodynamic* is one of the most palpable moves in Wildlöcher's books. The same slide is to be found in the report by the Inserm Collective (2004). Widlöcher is one of Inserm's expert consultants.
10. Hugo Freda, president of the ECF from 2008 to 2009, created the first of these centres in Paris in April 2003. The model was successfully exported to the main cities in France, the capitals of Europe, and countries in the New World.

Chapter Four

1. [As will be clear from the following section, the French term *la clinique* refers neither to clinical practice *per se*, nor to the building or institution that the English term "clinic" can designate, but rather the conceptual and classificatory exercise of arranging experiential phenomena in accordance with clinical signs. (Tr.)]

2. Known for his research on animal intelligence and educational psychology, the American psychologist Edward Lee Thorndike was a precursor of behaviourism.

Chapter Five

1. See the entry *épidémie* in the French dictionary *Le Grand Robert de la langue française Vol. III*, (Rey, 2001, p. 89).
2. To Braconnier we also owe the French biography of D. Widlöcher: Braconnier, 2003.
3. On this point, one may also consult: Sarfati, 1985.

Chapter Six

1. The 1893 classification of the causes of death is the forerunner of the *International Classification of Diseases*. Jacques Bertillon (1851–1922), aided by William Farr (1807–1883), laid its foundations.
2. Unless indicated otherwise, the quotations from this work are from the first chapter of Tome I.
3. *cf.* Crubézy, Braga, & Larrouy, 2002.
4. They mean "cognitivised psychoanalysis".
5. Furthermore, circular No. 2003–210, published in the *Bulletin officiel de l'Éducation nationale*, Issue 46, 11th December 2003, called upon employees of the education system to apply measures such as these. From the Chief Education Officer down to the dinner ladies, each staff member was asked to report anything they judged to be a "dysfunction" of a child or adolescent. Note that this age range covers the catchment population of compulsory schooling. It was specified that these "mental disorders" should feature in an obligatory mental-health record.

Chapter Seven

1. This chapter takes up part of Aflalo, 2009, published in Issue 37 of the journal *Cités*, 2009. The issue included a feature section on the ideology of evaluation.
2. See in particular Lacan, 2007.
3. On this point, one might consult Laurent, D., 2005.
4. Science shares this refusal of the body with the hysteric. *cf.* Lacan, 1990a, p. 19.
5. The trader works with the help of the one who invents the equations he uses (the quantitative analyst).

6. W. Edwards Deming, Joseph M. Juran, and Armand V. Feigenbaum (co-founder with Kaoru Ishikawa of the International Academy for Quality in 1971).
7. Elton Mayo was an Australian psychologist and professor at Harvard Business School.
8. *Modern Times* was the last film Chaplin made before the Second World War. It went beyond individual drama to stand as a harbinger of social tragedy: it was not about the destiny of one man, but the social system in its entirety.
9. Founded in 1946, JUSE was set up to study the industrial applications of statistics.
10. Manufacturing high performance weapons is another version of the taste for mortifying the living being.
11. Ichiro Ishikawa was the president of Keidanren (The Japan Federation of Economic Organisations) from 1946 to 1968. His son, Kaoru Ishikawa, a chemist and professor at the University of Tokyo, worked at Nissan and at JUSE (in Quality Control).
12. The invention of the psychoanalytic discourse is a response to the effects produced by the discourse of science.
13. Frederick Winslow Taylor (*cf.* Taylor, 1911) perfected a Scientific Organisation of Labour (SOL). His hierarchical management method left little room for the human being: he observed the workers, broke down their actions into their constitutive parts, and timed them with a stopwatch so as to work out how to reduce their movements to a minimum. The gains in productivity were spectacular, and the workforce was considerably reduced.
14. For a long time, the emperor's strong power slowed down the development of science in China. *cf.* Needham, 1969.
15. These remarks on the Asian theocracies and the differences between them draw on Max Weber's studies: *cf.* Weber, 1951; and 1958. Though these two studies date from before the period we are considering here, they helped clarify our view and we refer the reader to them.
16. On Japan's literary history, one may consult: Origas, 2008; and Lozerand, 2005.
17. On state religion, *cf.* Sueki, 2007.
18. Regarding the "cultural war", one may consult: Lucken, 2005.
19. Max Weber showed that capitalism is born of the ascetic religiosity of Protestantism which gave rise to economic rationalism. *cf.* Weber, 1930.
20. Among the different Buddhist sects, the Shin sect in particular showed an identity of way of life that was "in many ways similar to the occidental Lutheran manner" (Weber, 1958).

21. The French Canadian *qualimètre* and other such benchmarking tools were to ensure that the worker would continue to be constantly evaluated.
22. Shigeo Shingo was a Japanese engineer. Less well-known than Deming or Shewhart, he was one of the most important contributors in the domain of quality-control systems. A Japanese master of *kanban* (a productivity method), as an employee of Toyota he also invented the Single-Minute Exchange of Die system (SMED) which allowed for rapid tool changeovers, reducing production line stalls from hours to minutes.
23. Taiichi Ohno was a Japanese industrial engineer. He is considered to be the father of the Toyota Production System (Toyotism) whose main concept is Just-in-Time (JIT). *cf.* Ohno, 1988.
24. *Kaizen*: from *kai* ("to improve") and *Zen*. It corresponds to the US concept of "Lean Thinking" (five principles, set out by the Americans Jim Womack and Dan Jones in their book *The Machine that Changed the World*, which enable one to organise in a structured way the elimination of waste and the improvement of performance) and the French Canadian concept of VAP (Value-Added Production is an overall approach to manufacture that enables low-cost, high-rate production, whilst ensuring the highest quality).
25. The zero is the empty place, the emptied out place of the subject who "gets himself emptied" by language when he is represented by one signifier for another signifier. The subject-effect is an effect of emptying-out.

A few words of conclusion

1. *Scilicet* was the journal of the École freudienne de Paris. Lacan's introduction was printed in the first issue and reprinted in Lacan, 2001 (p. 291 for this quote).
2. *cf.* Miller, 2008.

REFERENCES

Aflalo, A. (1996). Psicoanálisis y Psicoterapia, ¿Qué curación?. *Uno por Uno*, 32: 44–49.
Aflalo, A. (2004a). Le colloque de Ch. Vasseur. *Agence Lacanienne de Presse*, Bulletin special "La guerre des palotins", 22nd March 2004, p. 40.
Aflalo, A. (2004b). Booz endormi et Lacan réveillé. *Ornicar?, 51*: 213–258.
Aflalo, A. (2007). Désinformation. *Le Nouvel Âne, 7*: 20.
Aflalo, A. (2008a). Le scientisme psycho-psychiatrique. *Le Nouvel Âne, 9*: 6.
Aflalo, A. (2008b). L'assassinat manqué : comment on devient psychanalyste au XXIe siècle. *La règle du jeu, 36*: 95–147.
Aflalo, A. (2009). L'évaluation : un nouveau scientisme. *Cités, 37*: 79–89.
Agamben, G. (2004). No to bio-political tattooing. (Trans: L. Thatcher). Available at www.ratical.org/ratville/CAH/totalControl.html
American Psychiatric Association (1994). *Diagnostic and Statistical Manual of Mental Disorders, DSM-IV*. Washington DC: APA.
Bensoussan, G. (2002). *Une histoire intellectuelle et politique du sionisme, 1860–1940*. Paris: Fayard.
Bialek, S. & Sidon, P. (2004). Les mauvaises manières de l'ANAES. *Le Nouvel Âne, 4*: 4–5.
Braconnier, A. (2001). *Tout est dans la tête*. Paris: Odile Jacob.
Braconnier, A. (2003). *Daniel Widlöcher*. Paris: PUF.

Briole, G. (2007). Le retour de l'hygiénisme, fiction de jadis. *Le Nouvel Âne, 7*.
Canguilhem, G. (1991). *The Normal and the Pathological*. (Trans: C. R. Fawcett & R. S. Cohen). New York: Zone Books.
Castanet, H. (2003). La logique de l'État stratège. *Le Nouvel Âne, 1*: 8.
Charrière-Bournazel, C. (2003). Attentat contre la dignité de la parole. *Le Nouvel Âne, 2*: 4.
Clément, C. (2003). L'horreur en somme. *Le Nouvel Âne, 1*: 2.
Cottraux, J. (2000). Therapies cognitives. *Encyclopédie Médico-Chirurgicale, Psychiatrie*, 37-820-A-50.
Cottraux, J. & Blackburn, I. M. (2001). *Thérapies cognitives des troubles de la personnalité*. Paris: Masson, 2001.
Cottraux, J. & Bouvard, M. (2005). *Protocoles et échelles d'évaluation en psychiatrie et en psychologie*. Paris: Elsevier Masson.
Cremniter, D. & Bognar, R.-M. (2005). Itinéraire d'un lacanien, Les derives de la psychiatrie universitaire. *Le Nouvel Âne, 6*: 20.
Crubézy, E., Braga, J., & Larrouy, G. (2002). *Anthropobiologie*. Paris: Masson.
Dazord, A. (1997). Evaluation des effets des psychothérapies. *Encyclopédie Médico-Chirurgicale, Psychiatrie*, 37-802-A-10.
Fédération française de psychiatrie (2003). *Le livre blanc de la psychiatrie*. Paris: John Libbey Eurotext and Fédération française de psychiatrie.
Foucault, M. (2006). *Psychiatric Power: Lectures at the Collège de France, 1973–1974*. (Trans: G. Burchell) New York: Picador.
Freud, S. (1900a). *The Interpretation of Dreams*. S. E. 4–5, London: Hogarth.
Freud, S. (1901b). *The Psychopathology of Everyday Life*. S. E. 6, London: Hogarth.
Freud, S. (1905c). *Jokes and their Relation to the Unconscious*. (Trans: J. Strachey). S. E. 8, London: Hogarth.
Freud, S. (1905d). *Three Essays on the Theory of Sexuality*. (Trans: J. Strachey). S. E. 6, London: Hogarth.
Freud, S. (1909d). Notes upon a case of obsessional neurosis. (Trans: A. Strachey & J. Strachey). S. E. 10, London: Hogarth.
Freud, S. (1915d). Repression. (Trans: C. M. Bains & J. Strachey). S. E. 14, London: Hogarth.
Freud, S. (1915e). The unconscious. (Trans: C. M. Bains & J. Strachey). S. E. 14, London: Hogarth.
Freud, S. (1916–17). *Introductory Lectures on Psychoanalysis*. (Trans: J. Strachey). S. E. 15–16, London: Hogarth.
Freud, S. (1920g). *Beyond the Pleasure Principle*. (Trans: J. Strachey). S. E. 18, London: Hogarth.
Freud, S. (1926d). *Inhibitions, Symptoms and Anxiety*. (Trans: A. Strachey). S. E. 20, London: Hogarth.

Freud, S. (1926e). The question of lay analysis. (Trans: J. Strachey). *S. E. 20*, London: Hogarth.
Freud, S. (1930a). *Civilization and its Discontents*. (Trans: J. Riviere). *S. E. 21*, London: Hogarth.
Freud, S. (2005a). Drives and Their Fates. In: *The Unconscious*. (Trans: G. Frankland). Penguin Classics, pp. 11–31.
Freud, S. (2005b). Mourning and melancholia. In: *On Murder, Mourning and Melancholia*, (Trans: S. Whiteside). Penguin Classics, pp. 203–18.
Georges-Lambrichs, N. (2005). Evaluation, mon amour. *Le Nouvel Âne*, 6: 16.
Ginger, S. (2004). Hommage a ma grand-mere ... *Le Nouvel Âne*, 3: 16.
Gould, S. J. (1981). *The Mismeasure of Man*. New York: Norton.
Gracián, B. (1681). *The Critick*. (Trans: P. Rycaut). London: Henry Brome.
Grauer, P. (2004). Epiphanie de la psychothérapie. *Le Nouvel Âne*, 3: 17.
Guedeney, N. & Guedeney A. (2006). *L'attachement*. Paris: Masson, 2006.
Guignard, F. & Bokanowski, T., (eds.) (2007). *Actualité de la pensée de Bion*. Paris: Editions in Press.
Hacquard, N. (2004). Compte-rendu 10h30-midi. *Le Nouvel Âne*, 3:15.
Inserm Collective (2002). *Troubles mentaux: Dépistage et prévention chez les enfants et l'adolescent*. Paris: Éditions de l'Inserm.
Inserm Collective (2004). *Psychothérapie: trois approches évaluées*. Paris: Éditions de l'Inserm.
Inserm Collective (2005a). *Troubles des conduits chez l'enfant et l'adolescent*. Paris: Éditions de l'Inserm.
Inserm Collective (2005b). Apport des marqueurs biologiques dans de la prévention du suicide. *Suicide. Autopsie psychologique, outil de recherche en prévention*. Paris: Éditions de l'Inserm.
Kovess, V. (1996). *Épidémiologie et santé mentale*. Paris: Flammarion.
Kovess, V. (2001). *Planification et évaluation des besoins en santé mentale*. Paris: Flammarion.
Kirk, S. & Kutchins, H. (1992). *The Selling of DSM; The Rhetoric of Science in Psychiatry*. New Brunswick/London: Aldine Transaction Publishers.
Kirk, S. & Kutchins, H. (1997). *Making Us Crazy. DSM: The Psychiatric Bible and the Creation of Mental Disorders*. Free Press.
Lacan, Judith (2004). Message de Moscou. *Le Nouvel Âne*, 3: 25.
Lacan, J. (1966–1967). *Le séminaire XIV, Logique du fantasme*. Unpublished.
Lacan, J. (1988). The family complexes (abridged). (Trans: C. Asp). *Critical Texts*, V: 12–29.
Lacan, J. (1990a). Television. (Trans: D. Hollier, R. Krauss, & A. Michelson). *Television/A Challenge to the Psychoanalytic Establishment*. New York: Norton.

Lacan, J. (1990b). A challenge to the psychoanalytic establishment. (Trans: J. Mehlman). *Television/A Challenge to the Psychoanalytic Establishment*. New York: Norton, pp. 79–106.

Lacan, J. (1992). *The Seminar Book VII, The Ethics of Psychoanalysis*. (Trans: D. Porter). London/New York: Routledge.

Lacan, J. (1993). *The Seminar Book XI, The Four Fundamental Concepts of Psychoanalysis (1964)*. (Trans: A. Sheridan). Harmondsworth: Penguin.

Lacan, J. (1995). Proposition of 9 October on the psychoanalyst of the school. (Trans: R. Grigg). *Analysis*, 6: 1–13.

Lacan, J. (2001). *Autres écrits*. Paris: Seuil.

Lacan, J. (2004). Entretien avec J. Lacan par E. Granzotto. *Magazine littéraire*, 428: 24–29.

Lacan, J. (2006). *Écrits, The First Complete Edition in English*. (Trans: B. Fink, R. Grigg, & H. Fink). New York: Norton.

Lacan, J. (2007). *The Seminar Book XVII, The Other Side of Psychoanalysis (1969–1970)*. (Trans: R. Grigg). New York: Norton.

Lacan, J. (2014a). True psychoanalysis, and false. (Trans: B. Khiara-Foxton & A. R. Price). *Hurly-Burly*, 11: 15–24.

Lacan, J. (2014b). *The Seminar Book X, Anxiety (1962–1963)*. (Trans: A. R. Price). Cambridge: Polity.

Lacan, J. (2016). *The Seminar Book XXIII, The Sinthome (1975–1976)*. (Trans: A. R. Price). Cambridge: Polity.

Lalonde, P., Aubut, & J., Grunberg, F. (eds.) (1999). *La Psychiatrie clinique: une approche biopsychosociale*. Gaétan Morin Éditeur: Montréal.

La Sagna, P. & Dewambrechies, C. (2004). La Sécurité "sociale" qu'on nous prépare. *Agence lacanienne de presse*, Bulletin special "La guerre des palotins" 14 & 15.

Laurent, D. (2005). Totale traçabilité. *Le Nouvel Âne*, 5: 6.

Laurent, É. (2007). Big Bonheur. *Le Nouvel Âne*, 7: 4.

Laurent, É. (2014). *Lost in Cognition, Psychoanalysis and the Cognitive Sciences*. (Trans: A. R. Price). London: Karnac.

Lazarus-Matet, C. (2005). Qu'est-ce que la Haute autorité de santé? *Le Nouvel Âne*, 6: 17.

Legeron, P., & Van Rillaer, J. (1999). Approche théorique des thérapies comportementales et cognitives chez l'adulte. *Encyclopédie Médico-Chirurgicale, Psychiatrie*, 37-820-A-40.

Leguil, F. (2004). Psychothérapie sur ordonnance. *Le Nouvel Âne*, 4: 4.

Lévy, B.-H. (1994). *La Pureté dangereuse*, Paris: Grasset.

Lévy, B.-H. (2008). Contre "la politique de civilisation", vive l'axe Lacan—Canguilhem—Lautréamont ! *Le Nouvel Âne*, 9: 42–43.

Lozerand, E. (2005). *Littérature et génie national*. Paris: Les Belles Lettres, collection Japon.

REFERENCES   153

Lucken, M. (2005). *Grenades et amertume: Les peintres japonais a l'épreuve de la guerre 1935–1952*. Paris: Les Belles Lettres (collection Japon).
Maleval, J.-C. (2003). Des vides juridiques aux évaluations. *Le Nouvel Âne*, 1: 6–7.
Matet, J.-D. (2004). La dictature du consensus. *Le Nouvel Âne*, 3: 8.
Miller, J.-A. (2001a). *Erótica del tiempo*. Buenos Aires: Tres Haches.
Miller, J.-A. (2001b). Lacanian biology and the event of the body. (Trans: B. P. Fulks & J. Jauregui). *Lacanian Ink, 18*: 6–29.
Miller, J.-A. *L'orientation lacanienne, III, 6, 2003–2004*, unpublished.
Miller, J.-A. (2004). Vous croyez que c'est fini? ... *Le Nouvel Âne*, 3: 4.
Miller, J.-A. (2005a). *El secreto de los dioses*. Buenos Aires: Diva.
Miller, J.-A. (2005b). A letter to Bernard Accoyer and to enlightened opinion. (Trans: A. R. Price). *The Pathology of Democracy*. London: Karnac, pp. 23–52.
Miller, J.-A. (2006a). Debate: Death to the shrinks? (Trans: A. R. Price). Available at: ampblog2006.blogspot.com/2008_06_29_archive.html
Miller, J.-A. (ed.) (2006b). *L'anti-livre noir de la psychanalyse*. Paris: Seuil.
Miller, J.-A. (2008). La sprinteuse clouée par ses escargots, même. *Le Nouvel Âne, 8*: 26–27.
Miller, J.-A., & Laurent, É. (2005). *El Otro que no existe y sus comités de ética, 1996–1997*. Buenos Aires: Paidós.
Miller, J.-A., & Milner, J.-C. (2004). *Voulez-vous être évalué?* Paris: Grasset.
Miller, L. (2005). Pour en finir avec l'utopie évaluatrice. *Le Nouvel Âne*, Special edition, 2: 7.
Milner, J.-C. (2003). *Les penchants criminels de l'Europe démocratique*. Paris: Verdier.
Milner, J.-C. (2005a). The Return of the Dangerous Classes. *Lacanian Praxis, The International Quarterly of Applied Psychoanalysis, 1*: 39–40.
Milner, J.-C. (2005b). *La politique des choses*. Paris: Navarin.
Mirabel-Sarron, C. & Vera, L. (1997). Techniques de thérapies comportementales, *Encyclopédie Médico-Chirurgicale, Psychiatrie*, 37-820-A-45.
Miremont, J., Sternschuss-Angel, S., Neuburger, R., Segond, P. (1990). Therapies familiales. *Encyclopédie Médico-Chirurgicale, Psychiatrie*, 3789 F 10, 4.
Murphy, H. B. M. (1977). Migration, culture and mental health. *Psychological Medicine, 7*(4): 677–684.
Murphy, H. B. M. (1982). *Comparative Psychiatry. The International and Intercultural Distribution of Mental Illness*. Berlin/Heidelberg/New York: Springer-Verlag.
Needham, J. (1969). *The Grand Titration: Science and Society in East and West*. London: Allen & Unwin.
Normand, M. (2004). Une grêle de rapports pour notre santé. *Le Nouvel Âne*, 3: 6–7.

Ohno, T. (1988). *Toyota Production System: beyond large-scale production*. Portland, OR: Productivity Press.
Origas, J.-J. (2008). *La lampe d'Akutagawa*. Paris: Les Belles Lettres (collection Japon).
Pichot, P., & Allilaire, J.-F. (2003). Sur la pratique de la psychothérapie. *Bulletin de l'Académie nationale de médecine, 187*(6): 1191–1195.
Plantade, A. (2004). Lettre ouverte au Pr. Brechot, directeur de l'Inserm. Available at: forumdespsychiatres.org.
Quételet, A. (1969). *A Treatise on Man and the Development of his Faculties; a facsimile reproduction of the English translation of 1842, with an introduction by S. Diamond*. Gainesville, FL: Scholars' Facsimiles & Reprints.
Regnault, F. (2003). *Notre objet a*. Paris: Verdier.
Rey, A. (ed.) (2001). *Le Grand Robert de la langue française*. Paris: Dictionnaire Le Robert.
Roudinesco, É. (2004). *Le patient, le thérapeute et l'État*. Paris: Fayard.
Roudinesco, É. (2005). *Pourquoi tant de haine? Anatomie du Livre noir de la psychanalyse*. Paris: Navarin.
Sarfati, G.-E. (1985). *La Nation captive. Sur la question juive en URSS*. Paris: Nouvelle Cité, Rencontres.
Seizelet, É., & Serra, R. (2009). *Le pacifisme a l'épreuve. Le Japon et son armée*. Paris: Les Belles Lettres (collection Japon).
Shewhart, W. A. (1939). *Statistical Method from the Viewpoint of Quality Control*. Washington DC: Graduate School, U.S. Department of Agriculture.
Skinner, B. F. (1948). *Walden Two*. New York: Macmillan.
Sollers, P. (2003). Chers psychanalystes. *Le Nouvel Âne, 2*: 2–3.
Sollers, P. (2004). *Le Saint-Âne*. Paris: Verdier.
Sueki, F. (2007). La place du bouddhisme dans la modernisation du Japon. *Japon pluriel, 7*: 22–36.
Taylor, F. W. (1911). *The Principles of Scientific Management*. New York: Harper & Row.
Victoria, B. D. (2006). *Zen at War, 1868–1945*. Lanham, Maryland: Rowman & Littlefield (Second edition).
Wartel, R. (2004). Lire le Cléry-Melin plume à la main. *Le Nouvel Âne, 3*: 13.
Weber, M. (1930). *The Protestant Ethic and the Spirit of Capitalism*. (Trans: T. Parsons & A. Giddens). London/Boston: Unwin Hyman.
Weber, M. (1951). *The Religion of China: Confucianism and Taoism*. (Trans: H. H. Gerth). New York: The Free Press.
Weber, M. (1958). *The Religion of India: The Sociology of Hinduism and Buddhism*. (Trans: H. H. Gerth & D. Martindale). New York: The Free Press.
Widlöcher, D. (1962). *Le psychodrame chez l'enfant*. Paris: PUF.
Widlöcher, D. (1986). *Métapsychologie du sens*. Paris: PUF.

Widlöcher, D. (ed.) (1994). *Traité de psychopathologie*. Paris: PUF.
Widlöcher, D. (1995). *La logique de la dépression*. Paris: Fayard.
Widlöcher, D. (1996). *Les nouvelles cartes de la psychanalyse*. Paris: Odile Jacob.
Widlöcher, D. (2000). Amour primaire et sexualité infantile. *Sexualité infantile et attachement*, edited by Widlöcher, D. Paris: PUF.
Widlöcher, D. (2003). *La psychanalyse en dialogue*. Paris: Odile Jacob.
Widlöcher, D. (2008). Le débat en psychanalyse. *Les psychanalystes savent-ils débattre?*, D. Widlöcher (ed.), Paris: Odile Jacob, pp. 11–20.
Widlöcher, D. & Hardy, M.-C. (1991). *La dépression*. Paris: Hermann.
Widlöcher, D. & Miller, J.-A. (2002). *L'avenir de la psychanalyse*. Paris: Le cavalier bleu.
Zarka, Y.-C. (2003). De l'arbitraire légal dans les démocraties. *Le Nouvel Âne*, 1: 3.

INDEX

Abenhaïm, Lucien 8, 90
abnormality, *see* mental abnormality
academic psychiatry *see* psychiatry
Académie Nationale de medicine 7
Accoyer, Bernard xiii, 5–6, 9
Accoyer Bill (Amendment 336/
 Article 52) xiii, 1–2, 5–14, 16,
 89–90, 97, 113–114, 135–136,
 141, 144n
affect 25, 42–45
 see also anxiety; chagrin
Aflalo, Agnès xiii–xiv, xvi, 11, 29, 73,
 144n, 146n
Agamben, Giorgio
 "No to bio-political tattooing" 99
Allilaire, Jean-François 6–8, 11, 15
American Psychiatric Association
 (APA) 62, 104
 see also Diagnostic and Statistical
 Manual of Mental Disorders
 (DSM)

analyst's desire *see* desire
analytic act 49–50, 52,
 140
anorexia 37, 40, 55
Ansermet, François 114
anthropobiology 112
 see also evolutionary psychology;
 sociobiology
anti-depressants 46–47, 63
anxiety 25, 33, 42–46, 53, 61, 63,
 75–76, 138, 145n
 see also castration, castration
 anxiety
arachnophobia *see* phobia
Aristotle xvi, 86–87, 124
Association lacanienne internationale
 (ALI) 6
Association psychanalytique de
 France (APF) 6
Aubut, Jocelyn 15, 87, 99, 107–113
Auschwitz 98

automobile industry 22–23, 120, 140
    see also Toyota
auto-suggestion see suggestion

Bachelot, Roselyne 10, 12, 131, 144n
Bacteria 81–82, 85, 104
Balzac, Honoré de
    La Cousine Bette 58
Bas, Philippe 10
Bayrou, François 4
behaviourism 74, 76, 108, 112, 123, 146n
Bensoussan, Georges
    Une histoire intellectuelle et politique du sionisme, 1860–1940 97–99
Bentham, Jeremy 84
    Panopticon 28
bereavement see mourning
Bergson, Henri 71
Bernard, Claude 28
Bertillon, Jacques 103, 146n
Bertrand, Xavier 9–10
Bialek, Sophie 4, 114
Big Five personality traits 73
biology 37–39, 44, 52, 64, 67, 88, 91, 95, 110–112, 115–116, 145n
biomarkers 87, 110
biopsychosocial model 8, 14–15, 17, 45–46, 55, 64, 88–89, 99, 105–107, 109, 112, 115–116
    see also psychiatry, academic psychiatry
bioreligion 15, 105, 116
Birnbaum, Jean 5
Blackburn, Ivy Marie 75, 141
Bleuler, Paul Eugen 54
Bouvard, Martine 14, 60–61
Bowlby, John 40, 45
Braconnier, Alain 88–89, 146n
Brentano, Franz 25–27
Briole, Guy 116, 136

Brusset, Bernard 6, 8
Buddhism 126, 147n
bulimia 40, 55

Camus, Albert
    The Plague 81
Canada 8, 15, 91, 94, 106, 113, 115, 128, 148n
Canguilhem, Georges 67, 115
capitalism, capitalist discourse 119–122, 124–126, 147n
Castanet, Hervé 117
Castration 43, 53
    castration anxiety 43–44
Castro, Françoise 4
Castro, Roland 4
chagrin 93
Chaplin, Charlie
    Modern Times 123, 147n
Charrière-Bournazel, Christian 4, 143n
Chirac, Jacques 101
cholera 86, 97
Churchland, Paul 77
Cités (journal) 146
Clément, Catherine xv, 4, 8, 89
Cléry-Melin, Philippe 3, 5, 15
    Cléry-Melin Roadmap 3–4, 7, 15, 89–90, 114, 117, 141
cogito 27–28
cognitive-behavioural therapy (CBT) 7–9, 11, 14–17, 22–23, 25–26, 31, 36, 40, 45–48, 55–79, 81, 88, 90, 93–94, 106–108, 112, 116, 127, 129, 136–142
    CBT ideology see ideology of CBT
cognitive psychology see psychology
cognitive science 22, 39, 47
Columbine High School massacre 11
    see also school shootings; suicide, murder-suicide

INDEX 159

Comte, Auguste 28, 106
  see also positivism
Constitution of Japan see Japan
Coordination Psy 5
Cottraux, Jean 14, 16, 60–61, 75–76, 138, 141
countertransference 51–52, 145n
Cremniter, Didier 114

Dab, William 7–8, 141
"dangerous classes" 91–95, 110, 112, 116–117, 141
Darwin, Charles 44
Darwinism 44, 110–111
  social Darwinism 111, 141
death drive see drive
Declaration of Independence (US) 144n
de Gaulle, Charles
  "Appeal of 18 June" 116–117
dehumanization 108
Delanoë, Bertrand 101
Deming, D. Edwards 123, 147n, 148n
  see also quality control, total quality control
depression, sadness 10–11, 45–46, 61, 63, 69, 86, 93, 120
  see also psychosis, manic-depression; psychosis, melancholia; mourning
Descartes, René 28
  see also cogito
desire 2, 4, 11, 25–33, 37, 41, 46, 50–51, 53–54, 71, 78, 83, 86, 124, 128, 130, 138, 140, 145n
  analyst's desire 52
deviation see mental deviation
Dewambrechies, Carole 107
Diafoirus, Thomas see Molière, *Le Malade imaginaire*

Diagnostic and Statistical Manual of Mental Disorders (DSM) 12, 62–64, 68, 86, 88, 93, 103–105, 107, 139
  see also American Psychiatric Association (APA)
Di Ciaccia, Antonio 115
Diotima of Mantinea 30
  see also Plato, *The Symposium*
discontent in civilization xvi, 11–12, 23–25, 70, 78–79, 92–93, 112–113, 119–120, 128–129
disorder see mental disorder
DIX-IT 4
Dombasle, Arielle 4
Douste-Blazy, Philippe xv, 8–9
drive 25, 33, 35–43, 78
  death drive 37, 40, 73, 108
Dutreil, Renauld 4

École de la Cause freudienne (ECF) 6, 10, 16, 145n
École freudienne de Paris (EFP) 16, 42, 52, 148n
  Scilicet 129, 148n
educational psychology see psychology
Ego Psychology see psychology
Elkabbach, Jean-Pierre 5, 16, 114
Empedocles 86
empiricism, empirical method 25, 28, 30, 32, 44, 56, 60, 64–66, 69–70
encephalitides 104
Encyclopædia Universalis 97
enjoy-meant see jouissance
Enlightenment 4, 14
epidemic(s) 55, 81–87, 95–97, 101
epidemiology 81–89, 92–95, 99–101, 108–109
  see also mental health epidemiology
Epimenides paradox 72

Erasmus, Desiderius
  In Praise of Folly 58
Esquirol, Jean-Étienne Dominique 83
ethics of psychoanalysis 31–33, 38, 50, 52, 107, 138, 141
  see also Lacan, Jacques, *Seminar VII*
ethology 40, 45, 74
evaluation xv, xvii, 4–5, 7–8, 14–15, 22–24, 46–47, 51, 59–64, 68–73, 75, 78, 81–83, 85–87, 89, 91–95, 100–101, 105, 107–110, 113–114, 116–117, 119–120, 122–128, 130, 135–136, 138–140, 146n, 148n
evolutionary psychology *see* psychology
Ey, Henri 111

Fabius, Laurent 5
Farr, William 146n
Favereau, Éric 5
Feigenbaum, Armand V. 147n
fetishism 41
Final Solution 98
Forums des Psyş xv, 4–5, 8–9, 90, 94, 99, 114, 144n
Foucault, Michel 95
  Psychiatric Power 100
Fourgous, Jean-Michel 4
Freda, Hugo 145n
free association (fundamental rule of psychoanalysis) 21, 50–52
French Department of Health [Direction générale de santé] (DGS) 7–8, 90, 135–136
French Federation of Psychiatry [Fédération française de psychiatrie] (FFP) 113, 144n
French Psychiatric Association [Association française de psychiatrie] (AFP) 6
French Republic 11–12, 14, 130, 139

French Revolution 57, 86
French Society for Child and Adolescent Psychiatry 140
Freud, Sigmund xiv, 6, 8, 11, 14, 19–23, 25–33, 35–41, 43, 45–55, 75, 77–78, 81, 83–84, 86, 115, 121, 124, 138, 141, 145n
  "Beyond the Pleasure Principle" 37
  Civilization and its Discontents 78
  "Drives and their fates" 28, 36–39
  Inhibitions, Symptoms and Anxiety 43
  The Interpretation of Dreams 29
  Introductory Lectures on Psychoanalysis 36
  Jokes and their Relation to the Unconscious 29
  "Mourning and melancholia" 45
  "Notes upon a case of obsessional neurosis (The Rat Man)" 26, 36
  The Psychopathology of Everyday Life 29
  "The question of lay analysis" 20, 115
  "Repression" 43
  Studies on Hysteria 38
  Three Essays on the Theory of Sexuality 30
  "The unconscious" 43
Freudianism, Freudian discipline xv, 16, 22, 25, 27, 47, 50, 54, 105, 113
fundamental rule (of psychoanalysis), *see* free association

Genet, Jean 109
genetics, gene, genetic programme 31–32, 45–47, 73, 84, 86, 92, 110–112, 116

Génisson, Catherine 131
Georges-Lambrichs, Nathalie 114
Ginger, Serge 143n
Glucksmann, Raphaël 4
Gori, Roland 136
Gould, Stephen Jay
    The Mismeasure of Man 112
Gracián, Baltasar
    The Critick 12, 144n
Grauer, Philippe 143n
Grunberg, Frédéric 15, 87, 99, 107–113

Hacquard, Norbert 143n
hallucination 46, 70, 83, 106
happiness 12–13, 39, 44, 73, 123, 144n
Hardy, Marie-Christine 45
Harvard University 111–112, 147n
Haute autorité de santé (HAS) 82, 114, 129
Heidegger, Martin
    "The Question Concerning Technology" 113
Heimburger, Anne-Lise 4
heredity 31, 44, 46–47, 83–84, 87, 99, 104, 111
    see also Mendelian inheritance
hermeneutics xvi, 25, 30–32
Hippocratic oath 76
Hiroshima bombing *see* Japan
Homosexuality 41, 64, 83, 107
hormones 46–47
Houssin, Didier 8
Hue, Robert 4
Hugo, Victor 98
Hume, David 44–45, 53
Husserl, Edmund 25
hygienism 15, 82, 84, 105, 111
hyperactivity 63, 68
hysteria *see* neurosis

ideology 13–15, 100, 104, 107, 110
    ideology of CBT 41, 47
    ideology of evaluation xvi–xvii, 146n
    ideology of perception 53
    managerial ideology 114, 128
    psychoanalysis as "ideology" 105
Imbert, Claude 116
Instinct 37, 39–42, 44
Institut national de prévention et d'éducation pour la santé (INPES) 10
Institut national de la santé et de la recherche médicale (INSERM) xv, 1, 7–8, 87, 135–142, 145n
    "Apport des marqueurs biologiques dans le cadre de la prévention du suicide" 87
    Psychothérapie: trois approches évaluées 1, 7–8, 13, 15, 135–142, 145n
    Troubles des conduits chez l'enfant et l'adolescent 129
insurance industry 64, 107, 114
International Academy for Quality 147n
International Classification of Diseases (ICD) 62, 88, 103–104
    see also World Health Organization
International Psycho-Analytic Association (IPA) 6, 14, 19, 23–24, 30–32, 35, 46–51, 54, 56, 139
    see also Post-Freudians
interpretation 24–25, 43, 50–52, 55, 129
inter-rater reliability 61
Irish communities 96–100
Ishikawa, Ichiro 147n
Ishikawa, Kaoru 147n

Jacques-Wajcman, Brigitte 4
Jakobson, Roman 29, 86

Japan 123, 125–128, 147n, 148n
    Constitution of Japan 126
    Hiroshima bombing 126
    Meiji Restoration 126
    Shoguns 126
Jewish communities 96–100, 111
Jewish quota 99
Jones, Dan
    The Machine that Changed the World 148n
Jouissance 22, 24–25, 27–28, 33, 35–44, 46–47, 50, 53–54, 60, 66, 70–71, 73, 76–78, 86, 92, 100–101, 117, 120–122, 125, 128, 137, 144–145n
    enjoy-meant 32, 41, 145n
    surplus jouissance 43, 121
    see also libido; object *a*
Jung, Carl 53
Juran, Joseph M. 147n
Just-in-Time 127, 148n

Kaizen 127, 148n
    see also lean-thinking
kanban 148n
Kant, Immanuel xvi, 28, 73
kappa coefficient 61
Keidanren (Japanese Business Federation) 123, 147n
Kirk, Stuart A. 63
Koch's bacillus *see* tuberculosis
Kouchner, Bernard 4–5
Kovess, Viviane 15, 90–91, 94, 96, 101, 141
Koyanagi, Kenichi 123
Kraepelin, Emil 83
Kubrick, Stanley
    Dr. Strangelove or: How I Learned to Stop Worrying and Love the Bomb 92
Kutchins, Herb 63

Lacan, Jacques xiv–xv, 3–4, 8–10, 13–14, 16, 20–23, 26–30, 32, 35–39, 41–44, 48–50, 52, 54–56, 62, 66–67, 77, 86, 117–119, 121, 125, 129, 139, 141, 143n, 145n, 147n, 148n
    Autres écrits 129
    Écrits 46–47, 118
    "Family Complexes" 109
    Seminar VII, The Ethics of Psychoanalysis 28
    Seminar X, Anxiety 30, 43
    Séminaire XIV, Logique du fantasme 53
    Seminar XVII, The Other Side of Psychoanalysis 124
    Seminar XXIII, The Sinthome 9, 42
    "Television" 39
    "True psychoanalysis, and false" 32
Lacan, Judith 115
Lacanianism, Lacanian psychoanalysts, Lacanian practice xv, 20, 23–24, 49, 51–52, 90, 101, 111
Lalonde, Pierre 15, 87, 99, 107–113
Lang, Lack 4
La Sagna, Philippe 107
Lausanne University 114
Laurent, Dominique 146n
Laurent, Éric 10–11, 56, 120, 144n
Lazarus-Matet, Catherine 114
lean-thinking 148n
    see also *kaizen*
Lebovits, Anaëlle 4
Leguil, François 143n
Le Guen, Jean-Marie 131
Leibniz, Gottfried Wilhelm von 77
Levi, Primo
    If This is a Man ("Muselmann") 98
Lévi-Strauss, Claude
    The Savage Mind 109

Lévy, Bernard-Henri 4, 9, 57, 100, 142, 144n
Lévy, Thierry 4
Libido 32, 36–42, 45–46, 145n
    see also jouissance
Lindh, Anna 101
Livre noir de la psychanalyse 9
Lozerand, Emmanuel 147n
Lucken, Michael 147n

Magazine Littéraire 139
magnetic resonance imaging (MRI) 31
Mahjoub, Lilia 6
Maleval, Jean-Claude 143n
Malthusianism 93
manic-depression *see* psychosis
Manifeste Psy 5
Marianne 135
Marx, Karl 121
master-signifiers 32, 128
mastery, "the master" 24, 54–55, 119–122, 125
    money-master 121
Matet, Jean-Daniel 114
Mattei Amendment 141
May 1968 events in France 62, 113
Mayo, Elton 123, 147n
McGill University 96
Meiji Restoration *see* Japan
melancholia *see* psychosis
Mendelian inheritance 99
mental abnormality 63, 68, 139, 142
mental deviation 68, 73, 109, 88
mental disability 94–95
mental disorder(s) 63–64, 69–70, 72, 84, 87–89, 92–95, 100, 103–107, 110–111, 141, 146n
    obsessive compulsive disorder (OCD) 46, 61, 71–72
    personality disorder 46, 72, 88
    psychotic disorder 61, 69–70

mental illness(es) 57–58, 65, 67–68, 82–87, 94, 96, 99, 116
mental health xiii–xiv, 13, 15, 23, 35, 59, 65–68, 77–78, 85–86, 88–89, 91–93, 101, 105, 107, 114, 116
mental health epidemiology 15, 85, 87–96, 100–101, 106–109, 141
mental health record 23, 142, 146n
mental normality 65–68, 73, 79, 88, 91, 139
mental retardation 103
metaphor 29, 32, 37, 42, 77, 86–87
metaphysics xvi, 124
metapsychology 28, 36, 41, 45, 49
metonymy 29, 37, 42
Miller, Gérard 4
Miller, Jacques-Alain xv, 1, 3, 6–7, 9, 13, 16, 23, 36, 38, 41, 48, 71, 90, 103, 120, 135, 143n, 144n, 148n
    Anti-livre noir de la psychanalyse 9
    Le secret des dieux 8
    "Letter to Bernard Accoyer and to enlightened opinion" 16, 103
Miller, Luc 145n
Milner, Jean-Claude xv, 4, 22–23, 92, 98
    Les penchants criminels de l'Europe démocratique 98
    "The Return of the Dangerous Classes" 92, 116
Molière
    Le Malade imaginaire (Thomas Diafoirus) 12
Moloch 8, 100
Morel, Bénédict 83
Moscow State University 115
mourning (bereavement) 11, 45, 93
murder suicide *see* suicide
Murphy, H. B. M. 96–97, 99–100

164 INDEX

Muselmann *see* Levi, Primo
Musil, Robert
    The Man Without Qualities xvii, 127

Nanterre massacre 101
National Agency for Healthcare Accreditation and Evaluation [Agence nationale d'accréditation et d'évaluation en santé] (ANAES) 82, 114
    see also Haute autorité de santé (HAS)
Needham, Joseph 147n
neurobiology 141
neuroleptics 47, 76
neurological symptoms 46
    neurodegenerative dementia 104
neurology 62, 104,
neuronal man 31
neurone, neuronal activity 11, 31, 47,
neuroscience 22, 25, 31, 39, 110, 117
neurosis 45–46, 63, 65, 70, 77, 110,
    hysteria 20, 38, 53, 55, 83, 86, 146n
    obsessional neurosis 26, 36, 46, 53, 76
neurotransmitter 11
    serotonin 46, 145n
Nietzsche, Friedrich
    The Gay Science 17, 57
    Twilight of the Idols 1
normality, *see* mental normality
Normand, Michel 143n
nosocomial infections 82, 101
Le Nouvel Âne 5, 11, 16, 113, 115, 117, 143n, 144n

object *a* 30, 42–43, 100, 109, 117, 121–122
    see also jouissance, surplus jouissance

obscurantism 3, 32, 112–117
obsessional neurosis *see* neurosis
obsessive compulsive disorder (OCD), *see* mental disorder(s)
OCEAN 73, 77–79
    see also Big Five personality traits
occultism 13, 51, 53
Ohno, Taiichi 126, 148n
Opposable Medical References [*Références médicales opposables*] (RMO) 113–114
Organisation psychanalytique de langue française (OPLF) 6
organism xv, 20, 27, 37–39, 42, 44, 65, 67, 74, 110
Origas, Jean-Jacques 147n
Ossicini Bill (Italy) 115

Pale of Settlement 98
Panic 61, 74
Pape, Gérard 4
paranoia *see* psychosis
Pascal, Jean-Charles 15, 90, 141
Pass 42, 55
passage à l'acte 11, 65, 93, 101
Pasteur, Louis 111
Pavlov, Ivan 40, 75, 89, 108, 137
Pécresse Reform xvii
Pelloux, Patrick 94
penicillin 84
personality disorder *see* mental disorder(s)
Petitnicolas, Catherine 5
Phobia 46, 69, 83, 139
    arachnophobia 76, 138
    "social phobia" 70
Pichot, Pierre 11
Pinel, Philippe 83
Pisier, Marie-France 4
placebo 140

Plantade, Alain 140–141
Plato xvi
  The Symposium 30
Plenel, Edwy 5
pogrom 98
positivism xiv, 25–26, 28, 30, 32,
  51–52, 106
Post-Freudians 31–32
  see also International Psycho-
    analytical Association (IPA)
poverty 92–94, 109, 141
preventive medicine 82, 85–86
Prieur, Cécile 5
Procrustes, Procrustean bed 25, 33
Programme for the Medicalisation
  of Information Systems
  [*Programme de Médicalisation
  des systèmes d'information*]
  (PMSI) 113–114
psychiatry 7–8, 12, 14–16, 45–46,
  55–60, 62–65, 82, 85, 91, 94,
  96–97, 100, 103–104, 113,
  116–117
  academic psychiatry (university
    psychiatry) 13, 15, 59, 62, 76,
    85–86, 88, 93, 95, 99, 105–106,
    107, 109–110, 114–115
    see also biopsychosocial model
  psychiatrisation of society 106,
    114–115, 130
  psychiatrists 2, 4–5, 11, 62, 64, 73,
    83–88, 90, 104–105, 108–111,
    114–117, 136–137, 141–142
psychoanalysis, analytic discourse,
  xiii–xvi, 1–17, 19–33, 35–39,
  41–43, 46–56, 58, 60, 76,
  78–79, 84, 94, 103–108,
  112–113, 115–116, 118–119,
  124, 128–130, 132, 135–142,
  145n, 146n, 147n
  failed assassination attempt upon,
    xiii, 1–17, 106–107, 119, 135

  see also Freudianism;
    Lacanianism; training of
    psychoanalysts
Psychoanalytic Centres for
  Consultation and Treatment
  56, 145n
psychology xv, 3, 25, 27–28, 31–32,
  44, 54, 113, 116–117, 132, 137
  cognitive psychology 137
  educational psychology 146n
  Ego Psychology 32
  evolutionary psychology 112
    see also anthropobiology;
      sociobiology
  "scientific psychology" 25
psychopathology 7, 14, 15, 55, 132,
  141
psychopathy 83, 129,
psychosis 46, 51, 55, 63, 65, 69–70,
  75–77, 83–84, 93, 96–98,
  103–104, 109
  manic-depression (bi-polar) 96,
    104
  melancholia 45–46, 53, 93
  paranoia 26, 70, 83, 93, 141
  schizophrenia 65, 70, 83, 93–94,
    96–97, 99, 103, 109–110, 140
psychotherapies 1–4, 6–7, 11, 13, 15,
  19, 47, 55–56, 90, 114–115,
  117–118, 130, 132, 135–136,
  138, 140, 144n
psychotic disorder, *see* mental
  disorder(s)
"publish or perish" xvii
puerperal (childbed) fever 81–82, 101
Putman, Andrée 4
Putnam, Hilary 77

quality/quantity xvi–xvii, 24, 44,
  60–61, 67, 124–128
quality control 22, 122–123, 125, 128,
  147n–148n

process quality control 122
quality circles 127
total quality control (TQC) 123, 127, 140
Quételet, Adolphe 67

Raffarin, Jean-Pierre 5
Ralite, Jack 4
Raynaud, Jean-Pierre 4
Real 9, 22, 24–25, 36–37, 39, 42–44, 54–56, 64–67, 75–76, 97–98, 124, 129
La règle du jeu (journal) 9, 57n
Regnault, François
  Notre objet a 100
rehabilitation 68, 70, 73, 88, 95, 112, 116, 139
Reinoso, Pablo 4
Renault, Alexandre 4
repression 21, 37, 43–44, 71, 78
responsibility of the subject 11, 14, 24, 27–28, 31, 78, 130, 137
revolution 57–58
Roudinesco, Élisabeth 4, 6, 144n
Rousseau, Jean-Jacques
  Dialogues: Rousseau Judge of Jean-Jacques 86

Sade, Marquis de 73
Sarfati, Georges Elia 146n
Sarkozy, Nicolas 10
Saussure, Ferdinand de 29
schizophrenia *see* psychosis
school shootings 11, 93
  see also suicide, murder-suicide
Schreber, Daniel Paul 84
Science xvi, 2, 11, 13–14, 19–20, 22–25, 27–28, 30–32, 35–36, 39, 45, 51–54, 58, 63–67, 69, 71, 73–74, 78–79, 81, 84–85, 87, 91, 101, 110–111, 116, 118–126, 129, 146n–147n

  see also cognitive science; neuroscience
Scientific Organisation of Labour (SOL) 147n
scientism xiv, xvi, 5, 11–12, 22, 24, 26, 28, 40, 48–49, 51, 53, 59, 61, 64, 78, 110, 119, 124–126, 129–130
Scilicet see École freudienne de Paris
Ségur, Comtesse de
  Mémoires d'un âne 47
Seizelet, Eric 126
Semmelweis, Ignaz Philipp 81
serotonin *see* neurotransmitter
Serra, Régine 126
Seuil publishers 8–9
sexual non-relationship 53, 70,
sexual/non-sexual drives 37, 40
sexuality 38, 42, 64, 70–71, 77
  childhood sexuality 30, 40
  see also Freud, Sigmund, *Three Essays*
sexuated being 68–69, 72
Shakespeare, William
  Hamlet ("something is rotten ...") 109
Shewhart, Walter A. 122, 148n
Shingo, Shigeo 127, 148n
Shinto 126
Shoah 2, 125
Shoguns *see* Japan
Sidon, Pierre 4, 114
Single-Minute Exchange of Die system (SMED) 148n
Skinner, B. F. 40, 75, 108
  Beyond Freedom and Dignity 108
  Walden Two 108
smallpox 86
social Darwinism *see* Darwinism
"social phobia" *see* phobia
Société de psychanalyse freudienne (SPF) 6

Société psychanalytique de France (SPP) 6
sociobiology 112
    see also anthropobiology; evolutionary psychology
Socrates 30
Solano, Irina 4–5
Sollers, Philippe xv, 4, 88, 99, 113
    "Chers psychanalystes" 113
    Lacan même 8
    Le Saint-Âne 99
Spencer, Herbert 111
Spinoza, Baruch
    Ethics 47
"steering state" 5, 117, 128
Stevens, Alexandre 115
stimulus-response reflex 45
Strangelove, Dr. *see* Kubrick, Stanley
subject-supposed-to-know (supposed knowledge) 21, 29, 77, 138
Sueki, Fumihiko 147n
Sueur, Jean-Pierre 4
suggestion 75–76, 138
    auto-suggestion 75
suicide 11, 65, 86–87, 101, 120
    murder-suicide 11, 87, 101
surplus-value 121, 128
    see also jouissance, surplus jouissance
symptom, symptomatology (psychical) xv, 11, 20–21, 24, 29, 32, 35–39, 41, 43–47, 50, 53, 55, 60, 64–65, 67–73, 75–77, 86, 111, 116, 119–120, 122, 124, 128–129, 137–140
    biopsychosocial "symptoms" 112
    Marx, inventor of 121
    medical symptoms 60, 85
    see also neurological symptoms
    Widlöcher as 56

syphilis 82–83, 103
Szafran, Maurice 5

Taylor, Frederick Winslow 147n
Taylorism 125, 127
telepathy 19, 26–27, 51, 145n
third-party payment schemes 107, 141
Thorndike, Edward Lee 73, 108, 146n
Thurin, Jean-Michel 139
Time magazine 108
Toyota, Toyotism 128, 140, 148n
    see also quality control, total quality control
training of psychoanalysts 13–14, 20–21, 52, 55–56
transference 25, 51
    see also countertransference
transparency xiv, xviii, 53–54, 58, 60–61, 69
trauma 42–43, 98
treponema pallidum 83
truth xiv, xvii, 9, 11–12, 37, 40–42, 45, 67–68, 71, 74, 76, 93, 137
tuberculosis (white death) 82–83, 85, 111
    Koch's bacillus 83
typhoid 86
tyranny xviii, 79, 100, 114

unconscious 21, 23–33, 36, 41–42, 46–47, 50, 52–53, 55–57, 60, 75–77, 86, 108, 138, 145n
    "structured like a language" xiv, 26, 29, 32
undecidable 66–67
Union of Japanese Scientists and Engineers (JUSE) 123, 147n
University of Tokyo 147n
university psychiatry *see* psychiatry, academic psychiatry

INDEX

Value-Added Production (VAP) 148n
Vasseur, Christian 6, 8, 144n
Victoria, Brian Daizen 126
Virginia Tech massacre 11
  see also school shootings; suicide, murder-suicide

Wagner-Jauregg, Julius 83
Wartel, Roger 90
Watson, John B. 76, 108, 138
Weber, Max 147n
Western Electric Company 122–123
Widlöcher, Daniel xiv, 6, 14–16, 19–22, 24–33, 35–37, 39–42, 44–56, 90, 99, 106–107, 110–111, 113–114, 138–139, 145n–146n

Wilson, Edgar Osborn 111–112
Womack, Jim
  The Machine that Changed the World 148n
World Association of Psychoanalysis (WAP) 13, 48, 56, 143n–144n
World Health Organization (WHO) 62, 68, 84–85, 91, 103–105
  see also *International Classification of Diseases* (ICD)

Zarka, Yves-Charles 3